SURVIVING
THE CLASSROOM

Tips For Motivating & Inspiring All Teachers

Rita B. Herron

Illustrations by
Clyde Carver

R & E Publishers
San Jose, California

R & E Publishers
468 Auzerais Ave., Suite A, San Jose, CA 95126
Tel: (408) 977-0691

Book Design by Diane Parker

Front Cover and Illustrations by Clyde Carver

Library of Congress Card Catalog Number: 94-28199

ISBN 1-56875-069-2

DEDICATION

To all the teachers worldwide who bless our children's lives with their love, patience, understanding, wisdom, knowledge and guidance and to my first grade teacher who made me feel good about myself and gave me an enthusiasm for learning.

Special Note:

I would also like to thank the many teachers who I interviewed and the countless teachers I have had the pleasure to teach with, especially those teachers who shared information, tall tales, and classroom ideas. I would also like to thank the children who talked with me and shared stories about their teachers.

THIS HAND I HOLD

by Rita Herron

This hand I hold I touch it now
       for all eternity.
The love, the knowledge that I share
       I give to you from me.

In hope that all you do and say
       reflects the lessons learned
and all the rewards that you receive
       are ones that you have earned.

I am your present teacher
       and your true friend
but when the year is over
       my love for you won't end.

For in my dearest memory
       forever you will be
and when you go I hope that you
       will take a part of me.

This hand I hold I touched it now
       for all eternity.
The love, the knowledge that I shared
       I gave to you from me.

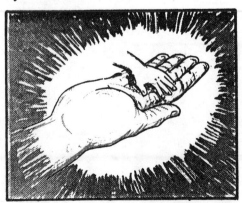

CONTENTS

CHAPTER 1
CALLED TO TEACH

Trumpets blast in the darkness. The gentle sound of the flute echoes in your mind, calling, calling, like the Pied Piper, almost hypnotizing you.

The melody lifts your spirit and you feel the *call* rise within you.

You've spent years attending school. Foremost, you have dreamt of graduation, but first you must choose a major. You've suffered through months of sleepless nights and voices fighting within you, voices telling you what you should do with your life, and finally the moment culminates.

You want to teach. You know it.

It is in your blood. It is in your skin. It is in your heart.

It was in your fingertips the first time you held a piece of chalk and in your eyes the first time you read a book. You smelled it the first time you inhaled the chalk dust as you banged the erasers together and you heard it when the screeching of fingernails on the blackboard sounded like a symphony to your ears.

It is your destiny. As sure as the phone rings forty five times a night from different salesmen, the call has come and you have answered. You have been CALLED TO TEACH.

MONEY IS NO OBJECT

"Yes, teaching jobs are getting hard to find. Schools and laws are getting stricter. The whole country is trying to upgrade education. However, there is always a need for qualified teachers. Openings do come up since our country is such a transient society.

Not a great salary, but the pay is getting better every year. All in all, a good choice for a major," your advisor told you, finishing his speech with a grin.

You smile proudly, your chest swelling with pride at your decision, dedication sparkling in your eyes. You quickly race out to buy your first tote bag decorated with apples that proudly displays the words *I Love Teaching* and purchase junk boxes to store all the pack ratting loot you'll be hoarding over the next 25 years.

Oh, well, money is no object, you tell yourself as the diploma you've long awaited is slipped into your hand. You've just paid your way through four years of college by working nights steam ironing clothes at the dry cleaners, your days flipping hamburgers and wearing a paper hat. You've worn the same three t-shirts and two pairs of jeans for the last four years. You've lived off chicken hot dogs, spam, potted meat appetizers, and Krystal hamburgers. Any salary sounds wonderful right now.

Besides, this is your calling. You haven't chosen teaching as a profession in order to get rich. You love kids, pre teens, or teens, whatever the age or grade you have chosen and you're dedicated to influencing the lives of the future of tomorrow. What could be more important than that? Certainly not money, you tell yourself.

"Teachers are some of the most valuable people we have in our society. They actually shape and mold our future by shaping and molding the children and leaders of the future." That was one day you didn't fall asleep during Mr. Doodlewire's speech.

When you heard that lecture in Teaching 101, tears had poured down your face faster than sweat could drip from your arm pits in a five mile race.

"Teachers are respected and admired in our country even though athletes, doctors, lawyers, and some assembly line workers actually make more money." Who cares, you thought! You're going to mold the minds of tomorrow.

Money is no object, you remind yourself as your 5'3" body shoots up through the 8' door and towers above all others. Your shoulder pads are bulging and pride spits from your lips when you speak.

You are a teacher now, and money is no object.

BEGGARS CAN'T BE CHOOSY

It's the last week of August and you're still unemployed. Panic grips you by the ankles and sends you into back flips. You're ready to save the world but someone must give you a little piece of land to work with.

Interview number 13, could this be your lucky one?

"We like your application. I see your preference is kindergarten. Unfortunately all our spots in kindergarten are filled. We do have one position in third grade. If you're willing to start there, maybe in a few years we can transfer and move you around," Mr. Lutz tells you.

"That'd be great!" you say, gulping at the thought of third instead of kindergarten. You can't believe it, your first teaching job. After meeting with 13 different principals, 5 different county employees and traveling to every school within a 50 mile radius, you finally have a dotted line to sign.

"Oh, I might add that our building is a little old and in need of repairs. We're also a little overcrowded."

"Oh," you comment, smiling and full of hope as you follow Mr. Lutz through the building.

"The county has put us to the max with trailers and your class will be here," Mr. Lutz says stopping in the hall.

You stop and try to hide the puzzled look on your face.

"Which room?" you manage to ask.

"Oh, well, it's not exactly a room. It's right here in this hall. I know it's not ideal, but it's pretty long, narrow but long, and you can have the whole space. There are only two classes on each side and they shouldn't disturb you too much. We've used it before and it's worked okay."

You stare at the long narrow hall and are speechless. You swallow hard and turn to examine the space. Then you spot something along one of the walls.

"What's that?" you mumble.

"Oh, that. That's one of the freezers from the lunchroom. I told you we're running out of space so it's here, just temporarily. Don't worry. The ladies from the cafeteria keep it locked and they usually just come once in the morning to get some juice and things out. They won't bother you."

You try not to look at your reflection in Mr. Lutz' bald head as he bends to stomp a cockroach. You turn away, hoping he doesn't notice the stunned state into which he has thrust your mind.

"You know I miss the days when we could paddle the kids," Mr. Lutz says." He laughs and scratches his rear. You stare at your shoes and groan inside. "Come on, let's go get the paperwork done," he says, turning and walking the other way. He rubs his round stomach and tries to tuck the loose shirt hanging out of his pants back inside. You grab your mouth with your hand to silence the shriek begging to escape when he grabs his underwear and pulls it above the edge of his pants.

You study the old wooden tables, worn and full of pencil carvings from years of use.

"How primitive," you think noting the cracks in the floor and the rips in the carpet. The room, well, the hall even has the smell of must and mildew seeping out of it like a house that's been locked up for ages.

Suddenly you jolt yourself back to reality and follow on the heels of Mr. Lutz.

It's third grade, not kindergarten, and you're in a hall, not a room. Okay, you can be flexible. Two of your friends still don't have jobs, you tell yourself.

"What do you think?" Mr. Lutz asks. "We're proud of our school and hope you will be too."

You force a smile and nod as he places the contract in front of you.

A hall with ratty torn carpet that smells like mildew and a freezer in the hall, you think as you scrawl your name across the papers. Not exactly ideal.

"I'm looking forward to it," you say, forcing a smile.

And roaches, you think. You shudder as you picture yourself sitting on the floor with the children and the roaches. Your hand trembles as you lay the signed contract on his desk.

Your first teaching job. You made it. You congratulate yourself as you step across the stained carpet, wondering but not wanting to know exactly the source and age of the stains. You head for your car and as you climb in and look back at the school you think. My first teaching job; oh, well, beggars can't be choosy.

"OH, SO, YOU'RE A TEACHER"

"Oh, come on, it'll be fun," your spouse says. "It's a dinner party."

A dinner party, you think, a chance to get dressed up, take your mind off the beginning of a school year and the three million things you have to do. Okay, you decide, as you step into your nylons and silk dress. The diamond earrings that you refuse to wear to school for fear of losing them in a can of paint dangle from your earlobes and your recent manicure shows no hint of the dried glue and paste you know will be flaking from your fingertips after a day in kindergarten or the pasty white dry skin that will accompany chalk dust hands if you're teaching another grade. You kick the tote bag aside and clutch your tiny sequined dress purse.

Hors d'oeuvres and candle light are the perfect backdrop for the business party you are attending and adult dancing mystifies you. What? No hokey pokey. Cultural shock and the reality of different worlds captivates you. A tall slender blonde woman who looks like she just stepped off the cover of Vogue magazine approaches you with her slender hand outstretched.

"Hi, I'm Dr. Morgan. I have a Ph.D. in psychology as well as a Ph.D. in Microbiology and I've done post doctoral work using the evolution of biotechnology as a major theme. I've studied at Yale and Harvard and did my post doctoral work abroad.

Now what is it you do?"

You shake hands, then stutter, trying to decode the jargon that preceded the introduction of your guest. "Uh, I'm a teacher."

"Oh, so you're a teacher. How nice." The woman's lips part into a polite smile as she turns away to greet an approaching colleague.

"Della, hi, darling, how are you?"

Ringlets of dark hair spiral around the woman's face and her emerald green eyes sparkle almost as much as the three kt. diamond nestled on her finger.

"Good, and you?" Della asks. Dr. Morgan nods and continues the conversation.

"Della, she's a teacher. Now what grade do you teach?" Dr. Morgan asks.

"I teach kindergarten," you reply trying not to stare at her picture perfect skin while you dab at your own nose, wondering if your make up is smearing into the beads of sweat you feel rising on your forehead.

"Oh, I've never understood how anyone could teach," the other woman says, giggling under her breath. "Kindergarten, that's not really a grade then, just kind of babysitting," the woman adds.

"Third grade, all you have to be able to do is add and subtract."

A short semi handsome man approaches, wine glass in hand, mischievous eyes darting up and down, undressing the other women as he closes in on their conversation.

"How sweet. So you just sit and cut and color all day," he comments, snaking his arm around the blonde.

Your jaws clench together and you force yourself to smile.

"Well, Della, here has her own design business. She's decorated some of the most prestigious buildings in the city," the man boasts.

Your face freezes into a polite smile, forcing yourself to suppress the four letter words that lurk in your throat like the dust bunnies collecting underneath your bed.

You instantly turn and scan the room. Another mother or teacher must exist somewhere in the room. At least mothers have been indoctrinated into the world of reality and realize that teaching is exhausting work. You spy another woman sitting in the corner and as you dart towards her, your husband grabs your hand.

"Here, Honey, there's someone I want you to meet." He drags you across the room and after fifteen stops to business associates, an earful of politics, the trade deficit, and marketing strategies, he finally deposits you in the corner, yes, in the corner, beside the other woman who looks and must feel as out of place as you.

"This is Tom's wife, Patty. They just had a baby."

"Oh," you say, smiling to yourself. New mothers are always full of conversation, in a language you can understand too.

"Hi," you say, reaching out and shaking her hand, "I have kids, too. Three of my own and then 27 more at school."

"Oh, so, you're a teacher," she says. You think you catch a tiny note of admiration in her voice.

"Yes, I'm a teacher."

An exasperated sigh escapes the women's lips.

"I don't know how you do it. I can barely take care of one little infant. I really admire teachers. I can't imagine teaching a whole group of kids and staying sane at the same time."

Your lips curl into a grin and you plop yourself beside the woman for the rest of the night. You've finally found someone who speaks the same language as you do.

WITH APOLOGIES TO NONE
Author unknown

Copied from a Columbia, S.C. Newspaper, January 1966

When I am introduced as a teacher, I am usually asked what I teach.

When I say "Kindergarten," I generally hear a very flat "Oh." I have never been certain whether it is an expression of pity, sympathy, disgust or perhaps disinterest. Always I wish I had the time to explain to them like this:

Yes, I teach kindergarten.

Where else would a handsome and very young man put his arms around me and say, "Do you know that I love you?"

Where else could I see a fashion show and keep up with the latest trends for the very young?

Where else could my limited wardrobe be complimented and my earrings thought beautiful?

Where else could I have the privilege of wiggling loose teeth and receive the promise that I may pull them when they're loose enough?

Where else could I eat a soiled piece of candy from a grimy little hand and not become ill? (They watch to see that I do eat it!)

Where else would the future look as bright as it does amid an energetic group to whom nothing is impossible?

Where else would I guide a chubby little hand that might some day write a book or an important document?

Where else would I forget my own aches and pains because of so many cut fingers, scratched knees, bumped heads, and broken hearts that need care?

Where else could I forget taxes and even the *State of the Nation* because Bill isn't adjusting as he should and other methods must be tried?

Where else could my mind stay as young as with a group whose attention span is so short that I must always keep a *bag of tricks* up my sleeve?

Where else could I feel so close to my Maker as I do each year when because of something I have done, little children learn and grow?

Yes, I teach kindergarten, Mr. and Mrs. America —and I—LOVE IT!

CHAPTER 2

ON YOUR MARK, GET READY, GET SET, GO

You glare at the calendar. It glares back.

10 days until preplanning begins, 9, 8, 7 . . . .

Should I be doing things ahead of time to prepare, you wonder? No, that's what preplanning is for, you tell yourself. Just relax, enjoy your last free week. You'll have time.

6, 5. . . panic buttons ring in your ears. Go see a movie. Go out to dinner.

4, 3. . . Insomnia strikes.

2, 1. . . Insomnia persists and your stomach is tied in knots.

0. . . You buy out the local drug store's supply of Kaeopectate.

The fact that vacation is definitely over strikes you like a bolt of lightning as your alarm clock thunders a bed buster to get you up and going and the empty blank pages of one hundred and eighty days in your plan book summon you to fill the empty spaces with exciting plans.

On Your Mark, Get Ready, Get Set, Go. The school year is beginning and the race is on.

INSOMNIA:
RESTLESS DAYS AND RESTLESS NIGHTS

Exhaustion and fatigue grab you by the cuticles and pull your fingernails into the quick but you still can not sleep.

All day long your head nods down to your chest just missing your sagging boobs and as you plow through your notes of things *to do* your face falls onto your spiral notebook, trapping your nose in the coils. In the car you are forced to open the window and turn the air full blast, blowing cold air in your eye balls just to keep your eyelids from super gluing shut. School is just beginning. Is this stress?

Night fall approaches and suddenly anxiety streaks through you, pumping your blood on high speed and making caffeine look like a sedative. You snuggle under your covers after a warm cup of tea and finally let your eyes rest. Your body stretches into a slumber but instantly thoughts go bulldozing through your mind.

Class roster, learn my way around the school, bulletin boards, stop thinking, GO TO SLEEP, you tell yourself, ... lesson plans, grade chair meeting, name tags, themes, centers. the grading books. . . . GO TO SLEEP. . . how should you organize the room, birthday charts, check out books from the library, discipline. . .

You sit up in bed and slap at the covers. Not again, you think. You have to get some sleep tonight. Tomorrow's the big day—pre planning. You have five days to get all that stuff done; five days. ONLY FIVE DAYS!

You pull the covers up around you and roll into a fetal position. You count sheep, toss and turn, count backwards from 16,000, fixate your eyes on the ceiling and count how long you can go without blinking (you're desperate; you'll try anything). Will you ever sleep again?

The alarm blasts. 6:30 a.m. You just fell asleep. You groan and moan and throw dirty socks at your spouse who is singing in the shower. Morning people are disgusting, you mumble, as your feet hit the cold floor and you feel your way to the bathroom sink.

The back to school blues jolts stabbing pains through your head. You splash cold water on your face and stare into the mirror. "IIIII!" you scream when you see the dark circles painting age lines under your eyes. "And it's only pre planning!"

PRE PLANNING: BEFORE THE WAR

You pick up your brand new tote bag, the one with the red apples and the bear on it that says *Teachers Are Beary Special* and lovingly trace your fingers along the words. It was a gift when you graduated and you've been waiting until day one of your real career before you used it.

You load it with a notebook, pens, markers, patterns, a couple of resource books and block letters to trace. You shove the poster board and collections of items for your centers that you've been saving for months; empty toilet paper rolls, egg cartons, yarn, baby food jars, and folders into the back. You pour a fresh cup of coffee into the *I LOVE MY TEACHER* mug that your mother gave you and head down the highway, eager for a week of relaxing and fun planning. You turn up the radio and listen to your favorite WEE

SING tape (or Don Henley's "All She Wants To Do Is Dance" if you're not quite ready to switch gears) and smile as you think of all you'll get done today.

You check your watch, perfect timing, even five minutes early. You grab your bag and step into your second home, at least for the next few months.

You enter your room, hall, closet or whatever corner you've been provided as a teaching space and stare at the empty blank walls. Where do you start?

You look at your list. Pages and pages of ideas and *to do's* are written before you. How should you arrange the room? What theme will you use? Name tags?

"Hi, I'm Jody," a young girl pops her head in the doorway.

"Hi!" you greet her.

"I'm going to be next door, teaching kindergarten. Maybe we can share some ideas sometime. You know about the staff meeting at 10:00?"

"Oh, yes," you say, jogging your memory. You know you wrote it down somewhere among the smattering of notes in your plan book.

"Well, better use this hour while we can. Sometimes those meetings take forever," she says and hurries towards her room.

Panic stings you like a yellow jacket. You grab your notebook and try to make some order out of your chaotic list.

Just when you begin sketching a design of how you want the room, Jody comes in. "Meeting time," she reminds you, thumping her watch.

You frown as you pass by a few rooms that look like they're ready for the first day. How did they get all that done? You follow Jody and hear a rumbling of voices as you approach the cafeteria. You spot groups of teachers huddled at the tables, talking, laughing, making notes. You slide into a chair and sit straight up. Alert, anxious and ready to absorb all the hub bub and excitement of the morning, your eyes rake over the staff.

"Hi, welcome back to all those *old*, I mean returning teachers and let me introduce the new people on the staff," the principal begins.

Pride swells like a balloon in your chest.

"This is our new third grade teacher, Miss Fresh. She'll be in the hall."

You smile and try to decide if the looks you receive are friendly or sympathetic.

Mr. Lutz scratches his round stomach while he talks. The buttons on his shirt look as if they're going to pop they're stretched so tightly across his midsection and his pants rest very low underneath his belly, the bottom of his pants sagging from his lack of a behind. He belches in the middle of his sentence. You doodle on your notebook and try to number the things you need to do while his hour long speech on his philosophy of life extends into a history of his childhood. He sweats and wipes his forehead with his handkerchief like a fired up preacher and when he starts naming the rules of the school you notice the *old* teachers wiggle in their chairs.

"I think we're here to learn and that's the only reason. Now when the boys and girls get here, they need to pick up their pencils and papers and go to learning. I've got workbooks ordered for the kindergarten (you see the teacher cringe), and a schedule ready for everyone else. Yes, Sirs, and Ma'ams, school is for learning, not any of that fun stuff like crafts and stuff like that. Now there's a few rules you know I'm set in cement about. You see I'm a bald headed man and I don't wear a hat and I won't have any of those kids wearing hats in my school. You understand me. Now if I can show my bald head then these kids aren't covering theirs' up. It's just disrespectful and I wasn't raised that way and I'm not having it."

You knew your class was in a hall but you didn't know it was set in the Dark Ages. You glance at your watch and can't believe that it's already 2:30. Mr. Lutz rants and raves, trying to explain in detail all the paper work he expects, then decides to read verbatim from the school handbook. You try not to watch his arms jiggle as he swings them wildly when he talks and you shudder at the perspiration rings under his arms that are growing like a major fog spreading over the country.

At 4:00 he finally catches his breath and leans against his podium. "Well, teachers, it's time for each of you to go to your own room now. Now go out there and make me proud!"

Each to his own room, you think as you drag your feet towards your hall. You look at your watch and at your *to do* list. You've certainly got to get your room ready for next week. Children will be coming in three days for registration. One day of pre planning complete and you've gotten nothing accomplished.

"Remember grade planning meetings tomorrow," one of the third grade teachers, Mrs. Corn calls to you.

You groan and go to close your door, then remember you have no door in the hall. Mr. Lutz' words keep ringing in your ears along with the sound of his belching. "Pick up those pencils and paper and learn," you think. Each to his own, you told yourself a long time ago when you tried to accept the different styles of teachers and people you met, but somehow you still weren't prepared for someone like Mr. Lutz. You watch the *old* teachers head for the door while you park yourself in the middle of your hall and start your day of pre planning; at 4:15.

PRE PLANNING
TIPS

- FIRST, make your list of *to do's*. Then organize and prioritize it. Order the items, listing what must be done at school and what you possibly could do at home. Check things off as you do them so you can see your progress and feel successful.

Your list should include:

Setting up the classroom: room arrangement, books, arranging materials, supplies, library materials, equipment, cubbies or boxes for sorting *to go home* papers and notes, coat racks, centers and special areas of room (time out, library, computer, etc.)

Theme classes: decide on the theme, the bulletin board, name tags, cubby tags, etc.

Bulletin Boards: a central stationary one for the calendar, weather, etc., and others for units, themes, and children's work.

Helper charts, leaders

Lesson Plans (Detailed first week, rough draft of first month), preparation of materials for first week

Your schedule and posting of it

Centers (Making and organizing your center chart or method of handling centers)

Behavior and Reward charts (if you use them)

Calendar (snack and special days)

List of Rules

Birthday Lists, tooth chart, Reading chart or other incentive charts

Bathroom, hall, and library

Making name cards

Setting up your files: children's files for office, children's files for room to store samples of work, your working files of ideas, themes, units, lesson plan ideas, forms, notes to parents, programs, etc.

Setting up and preparing for pre registrations; include files and emergency information to update, list for parents to sign up for room mothers, field trips, volunteers for helping in the classroom, crafts, computer, projects, etc., donations for PTA and memberships forms, note about supplies children should bring and what is provided, list of materials you might need such as craft supplies, kleenex, etc.

SETTING UP YOUR ROOM

Room arrangement varies according to the age of the children you teach, the subject, and your style of teaching.

Pre school—Kindergarten

You will need child size furniture, low tables and chairs, a rug area for group times and movement and lots of corners. Label the areas with words and colorful pictures to help children distinguish each area. Arrange quiet areas such as library, listening, and language arts close together and blocks and housekeeping, areas which tend to get more noisy, away from the quieter groups. However, don't put all your noisy areas completely together or your room will be lopsided and the noise from one area will jumble with the other and force the kids to be even louder just to be heard.

Areas for centers:

Library
Listening
Writing
Language Arts

Math

Science

Art

Sand and/or water

Manipulatives; puzzles, games, pegs, etc.

Computer

Housekeeping or Dramatic Play

Blocks

Pets

Utilize your tables for folder games and work jobs and use corners for science, listening, housekeeping, etc. Label areas and places for children to store items at clean up time. Use your rug for large games or for spreading out work jobs at center time, then use for story times, circle times, and large movement times.

Elementary Age

Children at this age enjoy having a desk and space to keep their supplies, work, and books. You can arrange in rows, although this is limiting or in areas or groups of four where children can work in pairs or groups. This invites a less formal atmosphere, encourages children to help one another, teaches them to cooperate, and helps them make friends. However, be sure to reward children for individual work and progress, not just for the groups. Changing the room arrangement periodically eliminates problems that occur with different children and helps all the children get to know one another, hopefully offsetting some of the cliques that form, personality clashes, and mixes the intelligence levels and abilities of the group. Small groups are helpful at times to individualize and centers help make learning fun and challenging.

Free centers such as art, library, games or puzzles also stimulate and reward the children who finish their work early. Keep an art center open with supplies at all times. Label areas for supplies for ease in putting things back.

DECORATING AND DESIGNATING AREAS

Bulletin Boards

Numerous books containing bulletin board ideas can be found at teacher resource stores or through catalogs. A few suggested ones are listed in the back section entitled *Suggested Resources*.

You should designate one board as a stationary board and on this display your calendar, center chart, behavior charts, weather charts, etc., things that will remain up all year. Hopefully, you'll have one or more other boards for unit projects and displaying children's art work. Utilize children's work and art as much as possible and display their projects to build their self esteem. If you're doing a decorative or theme related bulletin board, be sure to let the children help create it. Other bulletin boards may be used for teaching, displaying unit related pictures or ideas, or incentives.

Birthday Lists: all young children want their birthday acknowledged. Even if your school has restrictions on celebrating holidays and birthdays, you can acknowledge the birthdays. Cut birthday cakes or cupcakes out of construction paper and label with the month and children's names so you can acknowledge them at the appropriate time. If your school allows, let special snacks be a part of birthdays. Be sure to have special times set up for the summer birthdays. You may want to cancel homework for the class or individual child on his or her birthday.

Display a large tooth; let children sign or cut out small teeth and add to the chart every time they lose a teeth. Graph.

Reading Chart: use a chart or other system to list the books each child reads in the class. This reinforces reading in the class and is a reward for the child to see it posted. You can use a simple chart or use cute theme related ideas such as individual worm heads for each child which they add body parts (one per book) to make the worm grow, etc. Display so children can see their worms grow.

Organize the room so children know where things are and where they go. Label. Designate a place for everything; scissors, supplies, extra pencils, homework papers, blocks, games, etc. and be sure to allow for clean up time daily so children can learn the responsibility of putting things away.

Post a list or cut out buses and label with numbers and children's names to help them remember their bus numbers. Display so they can check it daily.

Post a copy of your class schedule so children can refer to it. Also designate the P.E. days (for wearing tennis shoes) or other special activities.

Prepare and label passes such as hall, bathroom and library passes. You can use paint sticks from a hardware store and paint different colors to help you distinguish which pass is for which activity.

Decorate your door to distinguish your class from others. Use your theme if you have one, something seasonal, or welcoming to school. Change this with each season, theme or month.

Let children help you take attendance and lunch counts by organizing a special section for this information to be displayed. Use popsicle sticks with a magnet strip on the back, one per child with his or her name on it. Mark off areas on the side of a file cabinet or other area such as Buying Lunch: First Choice, Second Choice, Sack Lunch. Children can check in each morning by placing their stick in the appropriate area. It gives you a quick attendance count, lets you know whose missing, will help them remember their lunch choices, and can serve as a graph or math activity as you count and compare.

For centers hang up posters or cut outs to designate areas. You can use numbers, shapes, colors, words or picture cues so children can easily identify areas of the room.

THEME CLASSES

Choosing a theme for your class will also depend on the age you teach. Young children love themes, cartoon characters, animals, silly names, flowers, etc. For young children, the cuter and more decorative the room, the more inviting. Fourth graders and up don't require cuteness, but still like color, some decorations, and variety. Make your room cozy and warm so children will want to come in. Then they'll want to learn also.

You can get a variety of different ideas for different theme classes from books offered at your teacher resource center. Remember, if it is your first year, start out simple and build each year. You may want to change your theme every year or every couple of years to give you some variety.

Suggestions and ideas for theme classes can come from the following or any idea you can imagine: bears, frogs, dinosaurs, bunnies, flowers, cars or trains, cartoon series characters or other tv series, etc. Older children may want to make up their own names for their class or small groups such as *The Crazy Eights, The Super Spiders, The Silly Slinkers*, etc.

BEAR THEME: make name tags out of bears, use different colors and name the colors when asking children to line up, count how many of each color, etc.

Pretend your rug is the cave and tell the children to go to the cave for storytime. As a behavior chart you can draw a mountain of poster board. Each child has a cut out bear with his name on it. He sits at the top of the mountain. If the child forgets a rule, his bear is moved to the grass, if he forgets again, it goes in the cage (a small basket). He can redeem the bear with good behavior. Reward the children who keep the bears on the mountain each day with a sticker. Give out bear hugs to praise children; a real hug and a paper bear saying *I Got a Bear Hug Today*. If a child collects a certain number of bear hugs he can win free time, time at the library, a homework pass, etc. Begin the week with your theme through bear stories and songs and other activities related to bears. For example, sing *The Bear Went Over the Mountain*, *Going On a Bear Hunt*; read *Corduroy*; have bear snacks; count plastic counting bears; graph; etc.

You can use this format and use frogs or any other theme. For example, the frogs could go to the lake (the rug), their carpet squares could be the lily pads, etc. You could use stars and let them reach for the sky, the carpet squares could be clouds, etc.

REWARD AND BEHAVIOR CHARTS

If you are using a theme, adapt your behavior chart accordingly. If not, use a picture or cartoon to brighten it up and then organize it simply. Write names and give stars or stickers beside the names for appropriate behavior or work completed, books read, etc.

When making these types of charts, be as specific and as positive as possible.

Adapt to your room and needs of your children.

Other Ideas:

Use library pockets and craft sticks. Each child may begin with empty pocket and get to place one in at the end of the day if work is completed or behavior is appropriate.

Cut out a colored car from construction paper. Label with each child's name. Have a red light, green light, and yellow. Each child should start on green. If he receives a warning for misbehavior, then he pulls a light and goes to yellow, caution. Another problem and he goes to red. If he continues to misbehave another consequence should be enforced such as loss of outside time, time out, etc. Establish these rules ahead of time and be consistent.

For rewards, each time you find the class or a group behaving or working in a positive way, give the class a compliment. Each time they receive a compliment, write one of the letters of the word *Compliment* on the board. When they have completed the word, the children can earn a pizza party or movie.

You may want to change behavior and work charts according to themes, units, or the seasons. In the winter, make a snowman for each child. Each day he gets to add a piece to the snowman (hat, scarf, mittens, etc.). When he finishes dressing him he receives a reward such as candy, small prize, free time, etc. In the spring, set up a baseball field, with each child having a baseball with his name on it. Each child can start on homeplate. With one warning or strike, he moves to first base, two strikes to second, etc. Three strikes, you're out! (Time out) You can also set your game up so each child gets a single, double or triple hit for positive behavior. Each time he completes the bases and scores a run, he gets a reward.

If you choose to give prizes or rewards, try to focus on individual behavior and efforts. We want children to learn to help each other, cooperate and work together in groups. It's okay to let one table line up first if their table is the quietest or receive a compliment, but to punish one child by denying him a prize or reward because another child at his table is talking is both unfair and teaches the child that even with his most supreme efforts, he may go unrewarded. If we want children to have a positive self concept, believe in him/herself as an individual and be able to stand up to peer pressure when it peaks, we must concentrate on nurturing the individual strength within each child. Children will undoubtedly learn in time that life isn't always fair, but as teachers is that our goal or is it our goal to teach and nurture each child as an individual? Think about it. If you received a bad evaluation on your plan book because everyone in the grade level didn't have hers up to par, how would you feel? So as teachers be as fair as possible.

Use a reward jar, grab bag filled with written rewards, or apron with many pockets and children can choose their own reward.

If you have problems with the class, call a class meeting and discuss. Let children offer suggestions for ways to improve, rewards, consequences, and how to help others.

FILES

- Set up files with emergency information, registration, etc., and store in the school office if possible.

- Keep a file for each child in your room and include samples of work all through the year. The child will enjoy seeing his progress later and so will the parent. Also keep art samples from each child and display in folder, book, or have an art show at the end of the year.

- Flag any folder of children with a special problem or allergy and keep this posted in your class.

- Make a file of forms for the office, forms for parents, forms such as *Cooking and Lending a Hand* so they will be easily available when you need them.

- Keep a file of notes you have sent to parents; some parents never seem to get notes so a few extra and a file to prove that you did send notice of certain things comes in handy. Also keep a copy and date any communication with a parent on specific problems.

- Keep a copy of all progress reports, weekly reports, etc., to show to parents.

- File all unit ideas or themes according to the unit. Include in that file language arts, math, science, social studies, writing ideas, music and songs, art ideas and samples, fingerplays, stories and books, etc. that go along with the unit.

- Create an arts and crafts file and a file for each season, unit, story, etc.

- File center folders according to unit, if appropriate, or skill if they are not related to unit or theme. Laminate folders for folder games and store pieces inside. On the outside of the folder label the name of the center using words and/or pictures or symbols to help children store the pieces when finished.

- Store unit, monthly or theme ideas, games, books in a box (if they don't fit in a folder), and label. Place the titles in a master file so you don't forget what you have.

REGISTRATION

If the children are coming to pre registration as well as parents, try to have as much of your room ready as possible. Their first impression as well as the parents' first impression is very important. Children and parents both have anxiety over *meeting the new teacher* so remember this. Make your room look as friendly, organized and inviting as possible.

If time or your school permits, send out postcards inviting the parents for pre registration or call the child personally. Children and parents will love the personal attention.

Dress professionally and be friendly. Remember to smile. Eye contact does count. Try to look at each parent and have a few minutes of brief conversation. Also, you must look at the children, get on their eye level and speak to them. Some children may be nervous and very shy. This is your chance to calm their nerves a little and establish the rapport you want to last for the rest of the year.

Think of a few questions or comments you can make the night before to prompt conversation. Asking about vacations, sports, etc., can draw the children into conversation.

If the parents will need to be filling out paper work for you, have an activity for each child to do such as drawing, puzzles, a fun information sheet, etc. Try to schedule and stagger the visits to give you time for each one but don't allow too much time or the boisterous ones and their siblings may totally destroy your room. Ten to twenty minutes is usually plenty of time. Also, you may want to have a basket of cookies or crackers near the door and cups of water. If someone lingers too long, you can tactfully invite them to leave by steering them near the door and telling them to have a snack as they leave.

Have short concise directions for the parents posted on a poster or the chalkboard so they know what to do in case you're busy with the kids.

Have your sign up sheet ready for Room Mothers, Parties, Field Trips, helping in the classroom, making games, etc.

Personally show the children around the room and tell them what they should do when they get to school the first day. For example, "This is the art center, games, computer, etc. Here is where your cubby will be to put your book bag and papers. We'll pick desks the first day. When you come in, the first thing we'll do is draw in our Journal." If children, know what to expect the first day or at least the first part of that first day, some of their anxiety will be lessened. Keep the morning activity the same daily or have directions written on the chalkboard so when children enter the room they will know what do do. Get the children busy as soon as possible. Have a name for your first morning activity such as *Eye Opener*, *Sleep Buster* or *Good Morning*.

EACH TO HIS OWN

The staff meetings are over but the grade meetings begin. Every boxer in his corner or each to his own room, they say, but you wonder if you'll ever get to yours.

The grade meeting begins with organizational tasks such as passing out materials, curriculum guides and texts but slowly disintegrates into bedlam as the mixture of personalities, ideas, teachings styles and methods take over.

"I think we should all do duck themes this year," the cutesy new teacher with the French braid says. You've heard everyone call her a Barbie doll and you can see why. Her slender legs, blonde hair and magazine chest should be in movies instead of a classroom.

"Duck themes in third grade," Ms. Stevens says. She has one year of experience now and obviously feels she has mastered the ropes. "The kids would laugh us out of here."

"I have a schedule worked out for everyone." "Here," Mrs. George says, passing out the copies and smoothing out the bun on top of her head.

Mrs. Frost frowns at the schedule through her bifocals. "But there's no outside time scheduled."

"Well, you think the kids really need it?" Mrs. George growls.

The other teachers exchange questioning looks. Apparently they understand Mrs. George better than you.

"Well, I want to do lots of art," you interject. "I love creative experiments with paints, craft supplies, different mediums of art. I did spaghetti painting one year and we painted feet prints when I student taught. The kids loved it."

"NO, no art time, except by the art teacher, " Mrs. George says, "See, it says right here." She frowns at you with a look of disgust.

"How about cooking in the classroom?" you ask, still pondering to yourself how you can fit the art in without getting fired.

"Cooking, we're not here to teach cooking!" Mrs. George exclaims. Her tone of voice sends goose bumps up your spine and you decide you're glad you're not in her room. (Oh, that's right, you're the teacher now, not the kid.)

"Cooking is too messy for me," Mrs. Frost says. "I like to just lecture."

Lecture in third grade, you think.

"Let's arrange our math classes," Mrs. George says.

"Math, do we have to group?" Mrs. Frost argues.

Soon, the discussion becomes heated and the grade chair person feels like she is negotiating a peace treaty between different nations. Every teacher, beginning or experienced, has his or her own philosophy, style and method of teaching. There are as many styles of teachers as there are kinds of kids you will face. You will find a variety ranging from the meticulous, compulsively organized, teacher unable to deviate one word from the lesson plans as outlined in the text to the over-zealous ambitious friendly sort who will try any and every new whimsical idea she runs across. Which one is better?

Obviously, the one that works for you. Brainstorming together, sharing ideas, methods of bookkeeping, discipline, ideas or ways of reaching students both academically and behaviorally, sharing games and centers, etc., make grade meetings essential. No matter how different the other teacher, you may learn something. Hopefully, somewhere in your education you'll meet a teacher who symbolizes the qualities and style you would like to emulate and you'll follow suit, adding, of course, your own unique disposition and flair.

Compromises may be in order and you may have to barter to have certain activities included (I'll trade one day of memorization for two hours of art). But when the grade chair person has aided the negotiations into some basic guidelines for the grade level, and you've signed the peace treaty and agreed to teach the curriculum ordered by the county, then it's each to his own. It's time for you to decide your own voice and style in your own room.

After all, the goals of the curriculum can be reached by many methods and if you think kids learn better from you while you stand on your head, eat potato chips and crush bugs with your nose, then you've chosen your style.

THE NEW KID ON THE HALL

You've colored game pieces until your fingers are numb. You've cut out laminated bulletin board characters until the floor has disappeared underneath the mass of plastic clippings. You've made name cards for desks, writing, cubby holes, bathroom passes, and labels for everything in your room that can not speak for itself.

You stumble around the school searching for the supply closet; oops, no that was the custodian's closet. Where did the principal say to go for the large bulletin board paper? The bookroom is close to the workroom, but which one? Do you sign the videos out from the library and the tv from the video closet or are they both in the library? No, it's not a library now, it's called a Media Center. There's so much to remember and you've heard so much in the last few days. You are the new kid on the hall (or in the hall) and you want to impress these teachers with your knowledge and professional attitude, not your stupidity. But you have to ask questions or you could spend countless hours tracking down these tidbits of information that everyone else already seems to know. It's not bad enough that you keep staying until dark when those other teachers are walking out the door at exactly 4:30 with their arms empty. You trudge home long after your stomach demands dinner, your arms loaded with papers, folders and construction paper. How do they get it all done?

Are they really as prepared as they look or have experienced teachers just developed an aura that makes them look more in control? Will you ever reach that stage?

You still haven't figured out where to store the 700 plastic strawberry baskets or the 6,000 milk jug lids you've been saving for the unexpected occasion when you just might need them. Teachers are notorious for keeping every form of junk they can find for recycling into art (they really began the recycling movement long before *Project Save the Earth* people caught on and took credit). Baby food jars, egg cartons, and empty toilet paper rolls are overflowing from the back seat of your car and your trunk is stuffed with a bean bag chair, pillows, posters and plastic stacking racks yet to be unloaded.

One day you'll look around and you won't be the new kid on the hall anymore. Next year some other idealistic soul called to teach will step into your tennis shoes and will knock on your door, if you're lucky enough to have one, and ask you questions every fifteen minutes like, "Where is the paper cutter and did I leave any of my crayons in here during the grade meeting or perhaps my brain?"

Then one day, after teaching for ten years you'll still be walking out the door with papers in your arms, and you'll wonder if it was just an illusion that those other teachers went home empty handed.

But until then, take a few tips and remember that at some point, every one is the new kid on the hall.

TIPS

- First of all, ask for help if you need it. Most teachers are sympathetic and understanding and want to help you. They've all been through it themselves, either with their first year of teaching or at a new school and they remember what it was like. They want to share ideas and may be stagnating in their own juices, teaching the same thing year after year, and they look forward to learning from the new kid on the hall, too; you.

- Take notes and a few minutes in the morning or evening to read over and review them. Mark off your completed goals, and make new ones for the day.

- Organize your notes and take notes on everything. Don't expect that you'll be able to remember everything at every meeting. It's impossible. Label sections for ease of finding things such as Discipline, Pre planning, Room Set Up, Videos, Library Materials, Texts and Supplementary Materials, Equipment, Forms, etc.

- Set up your filing system: pre planning notes, curriculum night information, handouts for parents, weekly reports, assessment materials, monthly guides, units, art, field trips, guest speakers, programs, etc.

- Keep files on everything, especially your lesson plans, so you can refer to them the next year.

- Set realistic goals for yourself. Get your class set up and organized first and your first week's lesson plans made. Then work on other things like new centers and art ideas. Plan to make one or two centers a week, not 20.

  You'll build your supply up over time. Recruit your children, neighbor's children and friends to help you make folder games or centers. You can even offer to pay young pre teens to color for you. They'll love it.

- And most of all, remember how it feels to be the new kid on the hall and understand this with every child as they walk into your room that first day. It will make undoubtedly make you a better teacher!

DRESSING FOR SUCCESS

Shove those jeans to the rear of the closet, that jogging suit in the back, that silk suit to the Church side, and those high heels to the top shelf. It's time for work and you want to dress for success.

What kind of wardrobe do you plan for sticky hands, runny noses, glue, magic markers, paint and bloody elbows to land on?

You stand in the mall and watch your sister head towards the executive department. "I need a new suit for the presentation next week," she says.

Yeah, you think, you're doing a presentation next week, too. Well, a storytelling session. But the things you need for your presentation can come from the dress up box in your room. Let's see, you need the wand for the magic fairy, the scarf for the old lady story, and the hat for the man.

"Come on, Sis, let's look," she says, pointing to a gorgeous silk blouse.

"Wouldn't that look great with the blue suit?"

You nod. "I don't think I'll be needing a new suit, though," you tell her, "unless, maybe it's a suit of armor or coveralls for fingerpainting."

She continues to search through the designer fashions while you steer towards the discount section. Economical, practical, comfortable and durable, you tell yourself. Oh, Heavens, you sound just like your mother!

But if you want to actually dress for success, then that's what you have to look for.

TIPS

If you teach young children, look in discount stores for inexpensive clothes, slacks, and loose skirts since you'll be spending much of your time on the floor or in low chairs. You won't be able to relax and teach effectively if you're guarding your sides for fingerprints and globs of green gunk which inevitably land at your thigh level. Flat shoes are a must for comfort and for ease on playgrounds when you race across the gravel to rescue the skinned knees and bloody noses that become an everyday part of your life.

Young children love bright colors and any outfit that features unit, seasonal or animal themes such as holiday sweatshirts, appliqués, bunny earrings, t-shirts with cute pictures, etc. You'll find your teaching wardrobe growing with every craft fair in town and your recycling may even lend itself to jewelry making projects. One Science teacher I know told a story of a child admiring her sweater one day. He finally raised his hand and asked her if the designs on her sweater were *paramecia*. At least she had his attention!

Be sure to encourage parents to dress the kids for success, too. Children who come to school in $95 dresses or $65 shoes, (it happens), can't relax or be creative if they are nervous wrecks guarding their clothes all day. Even though you can cover clothes with paint smocks from neck to heel, there are always those masters of messes who find ingenious and impossible ways of spotting their clothes. And it will undoubtedly be the child with the brand new white shirt or the one whose mother doesn't like you that crosses the line from fingerpainting to body painting in 60 seconds.

If you teach high school you may be proud that you look as young as your students. However, it's important not to dress like one of them. You can be attractive without looking like an old maid and your professional appearance and maturity will help you demand their respect. Also, if you're suffering from your midlife crisis, try to avoid dressing like you're sixteen (except when you're in your convertible or in bed with your husband) or you'll hear snickers of ridicule and feel even older.

Be conservative with make up and save your short skirts and flashy tops for the night clubs when you shed your blue jean jumper appliquéed with bears and your second personality emerges, forcing you to grab the band leader by his guitar and lead the audience across the floor in a dance train.

CHAPTER 3

HELLO CLASS, I'M YOUR TEACHER

"Hello, Class, I'm going to be your teacher this year."

Little eyes peer at you. Big eyes jeer at you.

Shy, quiet children filter into your room clinging to their moms like saran wrap. One mother stands at the door, staring at you just to make sure her baby isn't being forced into the dooms of destruction by an alien disguised as a teacher. She must have read the series of stories *My Teacher Fried My Brains* by Bruce Coville. She drags handfuls of tissues from her purse, clutches the door and begins to sob. Boisterous bodies rampage through the room like K-mart shoppers at a blue light special. In 20 minutes of free time, the room is destroyed beyond recognition, all those labels you painstakingly made have disintegrated into confetti, and you have an Excedrin headache, number 9,999.

If you teach older children, you find bodies larger than you staring at you like you are smaller than life, their eyes still glazed from lack of sleep. Adjusting to the new morning routine can't be done over night, you know. Looks of disgust pour from their eyes while they anxiously tap and fumble with their watches, sitting with one leg in the aisle, waiting for the bell to ring so they can escape to the snack machines, and the real reason they came to school this morning: to see their friends.

"I really wanted Mrs. Swift," you hear a girl whisper.

"Me, too, she's the good teacher. I don't like this lady," another child whispers.

"Yeah, look at those ugly shoes."

You look at your shoes. What's wrong with them, you wonder? You jerk yourself into reality and try to smile. You call the roll, trying to memorize the new faces, repeating names over and over in your head while you try to look all knowing. Thirteen blonde haired girls and eight brown haired boys. They all look alike. And the names; Chrissy, Christina, Chris, Catherine, Kathy, Cathy, Robert, Robby, Roger, and Roy. Your tongue is as twisted as your stomach.

"We're going to have a great year together," you hear yourself proclaim. You take a deep breath and try to remember the meditation you read this morning, but suddenly your stomach decides to do flip flops (you fight off the gas explosion you feel erupting from the rear, after all, wouldn't the kids just love to tell that story), and you break out into a cold sweat. A rash pops out on your neck and your legs feel like jello jigglers. You grab the closest chair to steady you and look straight into those peering, jeering eyes, "Yes, class, I'm your new teacher and we're going to have a great year."

FIRST DAY JITTERS: FUN OR FIASCO

You grab your plan book and take a deep breath into the paper bag you brought, just in case. Blink, focus, look at your plans, you tell yourself.

They're just children. After all, what can they do to you? You're the teacher.

"Establish order in the beginning," you remember the professor saying. "Set your rules." Your head swims with lectures but the sound of screeching voices from across the room jolts you into reality or whatever you may want to call your classroom.

"That's my seat," one child says.

"No, I was sitting there. Now move," another child insists. One body shoves another and as you watch elbows begin to battle your first morning jitters are dumped into the trash and you race across the room, jumping into your referee suit as you go.

There's no time to think and no time to sit around with the jitters. This is your class and you must take charge before the kings of manipulation and queens of bossiness toss you out on your diploma.

Fun or fiasco: you're torn with the desire to have the children like you and have fun the first day or the fact that you need to establish order for the rest of the year. After all, first impressions count and you don't want children going home crying the first day and not wanting to come back, but you know you can't be too easy or they'll mutiny in the first hour and turn you into mashed potatoes.

Don't feel alone. Even experienced teachers may feel a twinge of anxiety over that first day with a new class. New faces and names to learn and new personalities to try to mesh into one congenial group presents a real challenge. Remembering how mature the class was at the end of the year and how different they are at the beginning coupled with a new group of parents and the range of attitudes they have inspired in their offspring can hit you like a misguided hockey puk.

You study the schedule you've outlined in your plan book. For preschool it may look something like this:

Greet, Draw in journals
Free Play
Clean up
Group Time: calendar, weather, story
Small Groups
Centers
Music
Snack
Outside
Group

For older children:

Greet, seat work
Language Arts
Math
Music
Spelling
Lunch
Art
Outside
Social Studies
Science

Then you look at the blanks beside those times and hope you've filled them with appropriate, educational, and stimulating activities.

To make it all go more smoothly, use the following tips.

TIPS

Your first day and much of your first week will be for establishing rules, the schedule, and for getting acquainted. This is important and you can't by step the process or you'll suffer later.

Set the pace for the rest of the year by being friendly but firm. Although you want order, be understanding and slightly more lenient the first week. You don't want to frighten young children or send the obsessive over sensitive ones home biting their fingernails and starting sleep disorders but you don't want the gifted, children meant to be challenging types to think you're a pushover. Be pleasant but business like in starting the year. Establish rules and discuss them with the class. Make sure everyone understands the privileges, consequences and your system. It's better not to start reward and behavior charts for at least the first week.

Remember this is a class of real children with different personalities, not textbook descriptions so you'll have to adapt to fit their needs.

Start slowly, especially with younger children. Too many directions and too much information will only confuse and frustrate them. Introduce a few things at a time, preferably one or two new things each day. Don't introduce your rules, behavior chart, center charts and computer all in the same day. Also, introduce new activities one or two at a time. Putting out fingerpaint, scissors, and glue all on the first day can result in a fiasco as will allowing older kids to sit on top of their desks, bring candy bars for snacks and doodle all day.

Have every minute planned and OVERPLAN. Plan activities for getting acquainted, quiet seat work, centers, and a few fun activities. You won't get it all done, but if you have something planned, then if you end up with a few minutes to spare, you can easily fill the time instead of letting the time slip into chaos.

Get Acquainted Activities:

- Play *Jack Be Nimble*: put a candlestick on the floor, call each child by name and have the class recite the rhyme while substituting the child's name. While the class recites the rhyme, the child jumps over the candlestick.

- Play a silly name game or song and substitute names. For example: sing *Mary's Wearing a Red Dress* and substitute *John's wearing a blue shirt, Peggy's wearing a yellow skirt*, etc.

- Play *Who Stole the Cookie From the Cookie Jar* and substitute names.

- Bring *All About Me* items from home. You can do this as a teacher to introduce yourself, then let children do the same. Include pictures, favorite objects, etc.

- Feature one child or a group each day and display on the bulletin board.

- Game: Throw the ball or beanbag. As you throw it try to name the person you're throwing to. Or throw the ball or beanbag to music. When the music stops, name the person holding it.

- Interview: let kids group in pairs. The two children interview each other, then introduce one another to the class. Or let children draw names out of a hat or jar. Then they interview the person whose name they drew.

- Bring in baby pictures and display on a bulletin board. Use a current picture and let children try to match.

- Have each person introduce themselves by saying their name and a word to describe themselves by using the first letter of their first name. Example: Smart Susy, Radical Rachael.

- In private, tape the children telling something about themselves, except for their name. Play back to the class and let the class guess who is speaking.

- Accept the fact that if you use the first week, even two, working on establishing your rules and organization, then the rest of the year will go smoother. Fostering busy, active, and challenged children who know what to expect should be your goal and busy, active, challenged children who know what to expect breed very little trouble.

- Transitions to and from activities will take twice as long as you think. Try to make these go smoother by playing games or using signals to help you.

Tips for Transitions:

- For example; at clean up time play a record. Let the children know that when the record is finished they should be cleaned up. This gives them something to listen to while they work as well as a time frame in which to work.

- When asking children to line up use all kinds of fun games which teach as well. For example; Line up by colors of clothes you're wearing, types of shoes, colors of hair, eyes, the alphabet letter the child's name begins with, initials, last name or first letter of last name, children have to name a word that begins with a certain letter, tell the answer to a math fact, etc.

- Use these transitional times to drill spelling words, math facts, play simple games such as *I Spy*, word games, learn songs, fingerplays, review the day, etc.

- As each child lines up or sits down, have them say a sentence to add to a story you began.

- Calm active bodies by using exercises, fingerplays, movement activities, and rhymes, soft music.

- Warm up to physical activities by a warm up time—slow exercise, march in place, stretching, etc.

- Play the Quiet Game while waiting in line, waiting for the bell, etc. Quiet Game: one person is IT—they point to or name a person who is very quiet, then that person picks another, etc.

- Whisper names or commands—children must be very quiet to hear.

- Hold up words, names, cards or commands on cards or write on chalkboard.

Shuffling bodies from one place to another and learning the routine will be demanding so plan the work to be simple. You can increase difficulty in centers and seat work as time goes on.

Undoubtedly the children may go home the first week and when asked what they did, reply "nothing, we just walked up and down the halls and talked about rules. It was boring." While that is a large part of it, try to plan one fun or memorable thing for the day such as a favorite story, song, or art activity. Review the activities you did at the end of the day also. This will help them remember something to tell Mom, too. Prepare parents for these types of comments ahead of time so they will understand your goals and won't call you the first night saying, "My child is bored. He needs to be challenged more." (It happens!)

At pre-registration, when you show the children around the room, tell them what to expect the first day. For example, say, "The first thing you'll do every day is to get your journal and draw or write for a few minutes, then you may have free time." or "When you first come in, you need to get your supplies ready, sharpen pencils, and find your language book." For older children, have a worksheet on their desk or directions written on the board for a *get started* activity. Preparing them ahead of time will ease their first morning anxiety and will let them know what to do when they come in the door. The sooner they get busy and involved, the easier your day will go.

Be positive. Encourage parents to let children ride the bus to school instead of bringing them. If they must bring them, encourage them to let them out at the door and not to walk them to your room. If they don't, then parting may really become *sweet sorrow* for the mom and child and *real sorrow* for you.

For older children, display easy to read maps to help them find different rooms and areas in the school. Your school may want to name different halls using street signs. For young children, display pictures.

Decorate your door in a unique way and point this out at registration so children know to look for a squirrel and tree, a cave or something recognizable to provide a landmark for them.

Use a warning time and signals for clean up, time to finish work, getting ready to go home, etc., to help children be ready on time. Examples of signals include: play a record for clean up, when the song ends you should be finished; set a timer and display it so children can gage their time.

Have your room organized for easy access in finding and storing materials. Label with pictures or words and review the first week so children will learn where things go. This will save you many interruptions later when you're working with individuals or groups.

For older children, help them organize their note books and folders for different subjects. Encourage them to use homework or assignment pads to record and help them remember assignments.

When making lesson plans, you need to keep in mind alternating activities from large group to small group, quiet to more active, physical to stationary. By varying the pace of activites, children will be more attentive and alert.

Explain the areas of the room and your method of organization; supplies, centers and center charts, cubbies, boxes to collect homework papers, boxes or cubbies for papers to go home. (If your school doesn't provide these, use a cardboard shoe organizer. It makes great cubbies for papers and notes to go home. Label each space with a child's name.)

- Buy a bottle of Calgon and have it ready when you get home. You'll need it. And hopefully, as you lie back in the bubbles, soaking the muscles that ache that you didn't even know you had, and you think back on that first day or that first week and you wonder; First Day: Fun or Fiasco, you'll be able to smile and answer at least, "Somewhere in between."

BEGINNER'S LUCK

Beginner's Luck 1

Your day is perfect. You are greeted by fifteen smiling angelic faces. You said line up. They did. You said do page 50-355. They did. You said three hours of homework the first night. They smiled and said, "Sure, Teacher, anything for you."

Your schedule is perfect. You have a duty free lunch, a half hour break for Music, P.E. and Art daily, an hour of planning in the morning and the afternoon and you take nothing home with you.

Your room is perfect. It is huge, filled with supplies, toys, and games, and you have three windows across the back, letting the cheery sunlight and warmth filter into your classroom.

Your class is perfect. All the children are meshing just like the Brady Bunch.

Every parent of every child has volunteered to help in some way and your plans are made for the next three months.

You pull out your lucky nickel and rub it. You spot the kindergarten teacher across the hall, struggling to be heard over the clamor of the 29 rug rats playing dodge ball with their mats.

Beginners Luck, you think, or is it just you, such an incredible teacher. You pat yourself on the back and sink your teeth into the homemade chocolate cake one of your parents sent.

Beginners luck.

Beginner's Luck 2

Your day is a disaster. You try to speak over the clamor of the 29 rug rats playing dodge ball with their mats. You said line up. They tumbled on their heads. You said let's do some work. They threw legos across the room. You said storytime. They made up their own version of leap frog.

You said "homework". They said, "No way, Teacher."

Your schedule is a disaster. You try to devour your sandwich in the middle of 29 bodies throwing mystery food at each other, dropping silverware and stirring chocolate milk into their applesauce. You have two fifteen minute breaks for Music twice a week, and only one half hour planning period weekly.

Your room is a disaster. Your kindergarten room is packed, wall to wall children. Your supplies haven't arrived and neither has the furniture. Of course, you don't know where you'll put it when it does, maybe in the hall.

You have roaches, exposed pipes and only one overhead light.

Your class is a disaster. No one is meshing. Two children have wet their pants and one is questionable. One is having a temper tantrum while sitting in the trash can, another is standing on his head until he gets the tinker toys and two are eating soap. One refuses to go to the bathroom anywhere but at home and is sitting on his feet, holding himself and it's only 10:00. A whole group keeps trying to fingerpaint the chalkboard, two are engaged in a hair pulling fight, and three have lost their shoes and don't know where to find them.

You have already had one parent call and complain that you aren't nurturing his child enough, your para professional has strep throat, and one of your kids ripped your plan book into shreds.

You stare across the hall at the teacher with the big room and the class from Heaven. How did she get the room with the windows?

She must have something going with the principal, you decide.

Beginners luck, you think as you rescue the pet turtle from the Ninjas who wanted to see if it could swim in the toilet.

Beginners Luck.

THE HONEYMOON

"I now pronounce you teacher and class. You may all line up."

You hug the class. They hug you. You smash pieces of cake in each other's mouths and then the honeymoon begins.

Although the first week or two is filled with anxieties, rules, learning routines, each other's names, and practicing putting the toilet seat down, it is also filled with eager to please kids on their best behavior who have not yet become comfortable enough to test the boundaries of your patience. They watch you like a video for the first time, not like the reruns on television, and you study them in detail, just like you did the manual to get your driver's license. Polite and cooperative voices greet you, and yes, you thought one of them said "Ma'am".

They haven't yet stretched their tentacles underneath your skin and discovered the remote control button that switches your calm smiling face to one of total frustration, and you haven't yet discovered the second layer of skin that they are waiting to shed.

After all, it's your honeymoon. Enjoy it. How long can it last?

THE HONEYMOON IS OVER

"Pick up your own things.

Put the toilet seat down.

Clean up your space.

Chew your food with your mouth closed."

Nag, nag, nag. What's the matter? The honeymoon can't be over.

"Ms. Fresh, Johnny's looking at me," the tattlers start.

"She looked at me first," the whiner whines.

The quiet shy ones have shed their first layer of skin and have begun to slither out from underneath their rocks and slide into trouble. The do gooders and pleasers interrupt you every 15 seconds to show you how they helped you, and the boisterous daring smart alecks have discovered the remote control to your nerves and are playing Nintendo with your patience.

Now the marriage begins; the real test of compatibility, dedication and teacher strength. Will you pass the test or has your tolerance level plummeted?

"Ms. Fresh, why do we have to do this work? It seems stupid."

"Teacher, somebody farted!"

"SHEW-EEE!"

"Teacher, I don't have to if I don't want to. You can't make me."

Your blood pressure rises higher than your cholesterol level as you realize that yes, the honeymoon is definitely over.

THE OLD WOMAN WHO LIVED IN A SHOE

Thirty six kids in one room, you feel like saltine crackers packed in a box. If one more body tries to crawl in, the cellophane will rip and the bodies will come tumbling out in crumbs.

"Hi, Ms. Fresh," Mr. Lutz greets you. He claws at his stomach and smiles. "Another new student here."

You try to smile and bend to welcome the lost looking face that stands staring at her shoes.

"We're glad to have you," you hear yourself say, searching the cracker box room for an extra chair.

"The numbers are so high that we should get another teacher soon," Mr. Lutz says, "The other classes are at 34 so when we hit 37 each, we should qualify."

It might as well be 67, you think, looking at the crowded bodies hunting for a place to sit on the rug. You gave up the idea of forming a circle at 29, now row formation is the only way to go. Knee to knee, elbow to elbow, the little bodies beg for space to move.

Overcrowded, understaffed, overworked, underpaid, and out of space! You feel like the old woman who lived in a shoe who had so many children she didn't know what to do.

It's only one more, you tell yourself. Always room for one more just like the story of *The Mitten.* In your heart you know you have room, but another part of you knows that overcrowding limits your time, your energy, and your space, making it more difficult for you to do your job at your peak performance. What can you do? Whip them all soundly and put them to bed. Not an option!

You must stretch the cellophane and try a few organizational tips to help you cope.

TIPS

- Talk to the principal about extra teachers, a para professional or other kind of assistance, even if only part time and utilize that person for helping with small groups, preparing materials, etc. Parent volunteers or perhaps a local school with a program in work study, child development, or another related area might be able to supply inexpensive workers.

- Utilize parent volunteers on a regular basis. Schedule the parent for centers, small groups or individual help. Be sure to prepare and organize for the helper in advance to use him/ her for the most benefit.

- Discuss the problem with the class at a class meeting and see what ideas they have to help organize and solve problems.

- Extra organization will help you. Use cubby holes for notes, use checklists and cards for keeping track of centers, tasks achieved, etc. Also post checklists and teach the children to help record their work when finished, time on the computer, assignments, etc.

- Plan and schedule every minute. Always have an art or library center open for those who finish work early.

- For show and tell or large group times, divide the class or use small groups on different days for show and tell. For instance, girls could bring show and tell on Tuesdays, boys on Thursdays or assign 4-5 children each day. If possible, divide the class for P.E., Art, or Music. Half of the class could go to Music while half went to Art, then swap.

- Work in small groups and keep large group work to a minimum. Divide in groups and rotate.

- If possible, find an extra room, hall space or even a library corner to take small groups for quiet work and to allow more space in the room. Rotate these groups.

- Eliminate any unnecessary furniture. Use smaller chairs, cut mats in half, and use smaller tables if possible.

IT'S RECESS OR THE SOCIAL STRUCTURE OF OUR SOCIETY WILL FALL APART

"It's recess," you announce. Faces light up as bodies race towards the playground. Children who have never smiled or spoken in class laugh and chase one another. Monkeys hang upside down and release their hideous noises. Screamers scream and imaginations soar as children turn themselves into superheros, turtles, dinosaurs, karate kids, airplanes, and roadrunners.

Inside you scream and suck in the fresh air. You have a five minute chat with another teacher, interrupted only twelve times by various tattlers, but that conversation with another adult rejuvenates your inner spirit and helps you regain your momentum for the rest of the day.

Ah, recess, you think. It was delightful as a child, that time you looked forward to all day, that time when you could run and yell and make friends, and right now you're grateful that some very intelligent teacher who lived on the little house on the prairie invented it not only for the kids but to give herself a break, too. Teaching requires not only physical energy but the emotional energy of a mega person.

"Teachers, we're not going to have recess anymore," the principal announces. "The state has decided that we must have quality outside physical education time, so we will no longer call our outside time recess." (Another decision obviously made by someone sitting in an office somewhere who has never set foot in a classroom, has forgotten his youth, and is anal retentive, you think.) "Two days a week your class will meet with the P.E. instructor, one day they may use the equipment and the other two days you need to have organized scheduled P.E. activities."

"No recess," you groan.

"No recess," the children moan.

Organized time, you think. The children have organized time from the minute they walk in your door until the final bell rings. Everyone needs a break. They sit in assigned seats on the school bus, work quietly at school, can't talk in the hall, either whisper or sit at silent lunch tables, have a daily schedule posted on the wall, and now someone wants you to do away with recess; the only few minutes of the day they have to let it all hang out.

After all, how can the tattle tales develop their inborn skills and the whiners whine and run from the bullies if we don't give them recess. Band aid companies will have to declare Chapter 13 and boo boo boxes will join the ranks of the extinct. The nose pickers can't clean their fingers in the sand and the space cadets can't possibly come back to earth if they aren't allowed to fly. The boys can't chase the girls and the girls can't tease the boys. They will never learn to flirt and have the joy of gagging over one another and fighting off cooties from the opposite sex if we do away with recess.

Please, please, you beg, "Let's get back to recess or the social structure of our society may completely fall apart."

CLASS DISMISSED

The bell blasts.

"Class dismissed," you announce.

Children sling their backpacks over their shoulders and race for the door like a herd of cattle at round up time.

"Don't run," you hear one of the teachers remind the children as they scurry towards their buses. The footsteps and chatter of children anxious to get home looks like a stampede and you cringe when you think of the little bodies that might get crunched in the hall if they stopped for just a second to tie an untied shoe.

You gaze at the overflowing trash can, filled with yesterday's papers and today's mistakes, the broken pencils on the floor, the paint brushes to be cleaned, and the papers stacked on your desk, waiting to be graded. Your arms are weighted down with your plan book, monthly curriculum guide, resource books, IEP's, referrals, and papers to check but your arms aren't nearly as heavy as your heart.

Your mind keeps replaying the days events. How can you enlist more cooperation from Jack? Will Jennifer ever master the Social Studies material? Is Stephanie being challenged enough? And Colby; those definitely looked like bruises on his back. You noticed the way he tugged his shirt down when Ralph poked him and asked him what happened. It wasn't the first time you wondered about Colby. He was always so quiet, so well behaved, but he seemed so nervous. Sometimes his hands seem to shake when he wrote and he barely spoke and then only when directly asked a question.

Then Veronica cried all morning because of her parents' divorce. She also told you that her older sister, only 17, is pregnant.

And you thought you smelled liquor on Tony's dad's breath when he dropped him off this morning.

Your foot catches the door as you turn and look into the room for your final inspection for the day. Class dismissed, you think but is it ever dismissed in your mind?

The teacher's greatest flaw is also perhaps her greatest strength. It is probably one of the motivating factors that brought her into the teaching field; a big heart, a love for children, and a true sense of caring about each child, not only academically but on a personal basis. Those big hearts make teachers carry each child's problems home with them every night. It's hard not to. A teacher knows that parents love their children and are in charge of meeting these emotional needs, but for the year or short time that the child is entrusted to the teacher for a part of the day, the teacher also accepts some responsibility for the emotional part of the child. Trusting little faces look up to you and turn to you for help and as a teacher, you know you have to be there for teaching a child means teaching the whole child; mentally, physically, socially and emotionally.

A child's emotional state will affect his work and his behavior and you must take that into consideration. You must try to view the world from that child's eyes. If he is unhappy, hungry, tired, or hurting then those needs must be met before math or reading will seem important.

How do you balance it all? How do you dismiss the class when you go home?

It's impossible if you are a good teacher to totally dismiss the class and not think of them outside your room but if you've done all that's possible in the room and you've conferenced with parents, then you have to make an effort not to let those problems destroy your home life either. Take these few hints to help you cope.

HINTS

- Encourage parents to keep you informed of any changes or problems at home which might affect the child. Remember to be subtle, not prying. Explain that circumstances at home often affect the behavior and academic work of a child and you ask questions only in the best interest of the child. Even small changes such as a new room can affect a child. Others such as a new house, a sibling, sleep problems, bad dreams, illnesses, medications, death of a pet or family member, divorce, financial problems, etc. all can affect a child. Approach the parent with the viewpoint that you and the parent together are a team trying to create the best help for the child that you can.

- Try to involve parents in any plans or goals for the child. Keep communication open. Include the counselor at a conference if you feel you need. Try to steer the parent into channels for help if appropriate; for example, parenting classes, financial aid, etc. Also, listen to the parent. Sometimes you will learn a lot about the child, his personality, homelife, friendships in the neighborhood, etc. from anecdotes and stories the parent offers.

- Make a written plan. Keep a journal or book to record problems, your plans for action and accomplishments. Label with every achievement so you can see progress.

- Try to write down your problems, goals and plans before you leave school, symbolically leaving the problems there also.

- Consult another teacher, counselor, principal, or your director for advice and help with specific problems in a private conference, not in the teacher's lounge. Be discreet.

- Set aside a special time each day for homework and problem solving, even for worrying, but limit yourself. Then take a break, enjoy your family, a movie, a book, anything that is relaxing to you. Remember to *take care of yourself* and you'll be more effective with your own family and your class. You may have to train yourself to turn your thoughts to other things by using a time limit or a set time each day for problem solving, but try to do this or you'll find your nights are filled with worries, not the sleep your body craves.

- Exercise regularly. It's a great stress reducer, gives you more energy, allows you to let out your frustrations, and also is a great time for your problem solving or thinking.

- Take action if you need to. You may need to report certain problems to a counselor, child abuse council or other appropriate agencies. Work with these people to help benefit the child and aid the parents in learning parenting skills. Work with the counselors in your school to offer parenting classes and workshops for parents.

- Then finally, when you've done all you can do, remind yourself of that fact. Set realistic expectations. After all, you're just a teacher, just a human (although high school students would argue this point.) You may want to save the world, but realistically you can't, at least not all at once. So, just take it one step at a time. Remember good things come in little pieces and sometimes so does progress.

CHAPTER 4
NO STEREOTYPES, PLEASE!

"Class, remember, each child is an individual. He or she grows and learns at his own developmental rate. Be careful not to *tag* or label children as they may fall into the self-fulfilling prophecy category if you do."

You heard these words in a lecture in Education 101, a lecture you'd always remember. It is etched in your brain like hearts and initials get etched into trees. But you really didn't need to hear all that, you thought. Why would anyone label a child or group of children anyway? You're certainly an open minded person. You accept others as they are. You're going to love them all, look at each child as a challenge. You will respect, motivate, challenge and set goals for each child as an individual.

THE TEACHER'S OATH

Raise your right hand. Do you solemnly promise before rug rats, principals and parents of rug rats that you will love, teach and nurture each child as an individual, showing no favoritism or bias towards any one child or group of children?

"I Do."

With your degree in hand, I now pronounce you *TEACHER*.

Stereotypes—NEVER! Not you, you think.

Then one day, yes, one day you stand face to face with your class and after eleven straight days of being interrupted by the same child who has raised his hand forty seven times to tell you every detail of every subject you have discussed and who has corrected you at least fourteen times in one hour, you hear yourself thinking; "Aha, the genius, the little know it all, I'd recognize you anywhere."

THE GENIUS AND THE KNOW IT ALL'S

"Teacher, I'm a genius. I have an IQ of 185," the little boy smiles up at you as he adjusts his wire rimmed glasses.

"Oh, that's interesting," you reply.

"Yes, I just finished *Canterbury Tales*. I found it very interesting. Next week, I'm beginning a study of Shakespeare's influence in literature. How do you feel about his influence? And how do you feel about the new policies the President is proposing? Do you think we could set up a debate in the classroom to discuss the future of the tax deficit?"

You smile, a debate over Presidential policies, you think. What planet did this child come from?

You look around your kindergarten room at the sand table and fingerpaints and wonder how this one is going to fit in. What can you possibly offer this child?

"Well, I'm not certain about a debate but maybe we could talk about it sometime. Let's see what you might find interesting today."

"Teacher, I'd like to study the molecular structure of . . . "

As he speaks, he follows you across the room, trips over his shoestrings and sprawls on the floor.

"Are you okay?" you ask. He lies there limp and helpless and nods.

"Well, hop up and tie your shoes so you don't fall again."

"Can't," he mumbles.

"Oh," you say, smiling at him and extending your hand. Well, maybe, there's one thing you can teach him. He understands molecular structure but can't tie his shoes. It's a start.

"Teacher, that's not the right way," a little girl interrupts. She bends, pulls her shoe strings apart and starts demonstrating.

"See, my mama says you do it this way."

"Thanks, dear, yes, that is one way, but you can do it both ways."

"But this is the best way," she insists and pulls the other one apart and ties it. "See, it's faster."

"Let's go to the circle for story time," you announce, taking your place in the circle on the floor.

You hold up the book about planets and start to read. The Genius interrupts you to tell you details about the distances between each planet, the moons, temperatures on the planets, etc.

The same little girl who demonstrated shoe tying to you interrupts you to tell you that you mispronounced a word.

"It's snack time," you declare. "Everyone find a place at the table."

The little girl says, "Teacher, it's faster if you sit all the plates out, then cut and serve, instead of doing it one at a time." (The know it all, you say to yourself silently.)

The genius adds, "Yes, and with a cake this size you should be able to get 24 pieces, each a perfect 6 inch square."

Somehow you feel like you should go play in the block corner and let these two take over.

No stereotypes, you remind yourself. They're all individuals. It's a normal class filled with special children. After all, you're not really stereotyping. You can't help it because there just happens to be one genius and one know it all in your classroom.

TANTRUMS, TEARS, AND TATTLE TALES

Your IQ feels stunted and a little threatened by the genius, you finally admit to yourself and you battle daily to recover your wilting self concept from the clutches of the know it all who constantly corrects you. Just then, the tiny shy little girl decides to bring her second personality to school and cracks it open like a peanut shell.

Of course it all happens on Parents' Day when forty seven parents line your room to watch the music program you've been practicing for two months. She doesn't want to wear her costume, the one her mother stayed up until midnight hand sewing the night before so she throws it across the floor, kicks and screams and runs around the room. Her grandparents have just driven for six hours for this performance and plead with her to stop and wear the darling little costume. She holds her breath until she almost turns blue, then spits across the room onto the hat of the leading star. Next she dives across the costumed ducks, ripping the feathers from their costumes, and crawls under a table, knocking the whiner (Oops, you haven't met him yet) down on his head. There she proceeds to bang the floor with her fists and scream.

The mother looks at you apologetically and says, "She's usually such an angel. She only does this when she's taking medicine."

The whiner is still lying on his head, crying his pitiful grating whine, occasionally peering up from his folded arms to see if anyone is watching. He wipes his nose on his sleeve and sniffs so loud you could hear him in Jamaica.

The leading star of the program, the sweet little girl who turns to tears over flies being smashed, buries her face in her lap and explodes into sobs.

The tattle tale trio emerge to point at the nose pickers, the hair pullers and the Tooter (you know, the one who likes to teach everyone how to make farting noises with their arms).

The temper tantrum returns, her father dragging her by her collar, crosses her legs and refuses to move. Tiny tears can't get her breath and has zebra make up dripping off her chin onto her pillow case costume; the whiner is clutching his leg and groaning as if he needs surgery and the members of the tattle tale trio start tattling on each other.

"Welcome to our program," you say, biting your lip, "the children have worked so hard to get ready for today." You close your eyes and envision the perfect class. Then you stand back and smile and wait for the applause.

THE DO GOODERS AND THE PLEASERS

You gaze over at your class. The Do Gooders and Pleasers are sitting quietly, hands and feet folded, smiling angelically, watching the havoc, waiting patiently for the program and for you to gain control. You sense the wheels turning in their heads. "How can we help the teacher?" One is comforting Tiny Tears and one of the pleasers stands up and announces:

"We're ready to begin. Our teacher has worked so hard to help us. I think we should give her a hand." She flips her pony tail over her shoulder and smiles proudly, her little face beaming at you.

You pat Tiny Tears' make up dry. You calmly escort Temper Tantrum to the time out area and offer her a choice to join you when she blocks the flood gates and gains control. Then you motion the tattle tale trio to take their places.

The Do Gooders and Pleasers sit with their hands folded and their feet crossed, singing, taking turns for their parts, never having to be prompted or told, always eager and ready to jump in and help. They perform like little Broadway stars, bowing and taking an encore from the audience. The whiner limps on stage and mumbles his part between sniffles, his chin quivering as he speaks.

All in all, the program goes okay. It doesn't seem to matter to the parents that the Genius sang the chorus in French, the Know it All stopped the music teacher once to tell her she was playing the piano in the wrong key, and the Do Gooders and Pleasers made you look like you left your head in Omaha. Once the singing began, the parents were enthralled in watching and videotaping their special little angels. Mothers oohed and aaahed and the fathers seemed to have their arms superglued to their video cameras. By the time the program was over, the beginning havoc was forgotten and proud mothers were ready to seize the yellow pages and hunt for the phone number for *Search for the Stars.* You beamed with pride. Afterall, putting together a performance for parents was a major undertaking and you deserve a little praise. And it wasn't until you watched the video later that week that you realized the Space Cadet was sitting on the front row with his back to the audience for the entire show.

WHINERS, SMART ALECKS, AND SPACE CADETS

Finally you think it's safe and your day may be restored to some semblance of normality. The parents have said their goodbyes. The tears and tantrums have subsided. You are lining the children up to go to P.E. and grab yourself a quick much needed bathroom break (you even penciled it in on the calendar: Wednesday, 2:00 bathroom), but relentlessly once again the whiner begins.

He clutches his leg and you see the green junk ooze down the side of his nose. His stretched out drawl chimes, "Teacher, my leg hurts and my foot hurts. My toenail hurts. I can't do P.E."

"Oh, toenail, smo-nail, you're a little rat's tail. Something always hurts on you," the Smart Aleck smirks.

"He's making fun of me. Teacher, it really does hurt." His eyes fill with tears and he wretches back and forth, rubbing his toe as if he is in agony.

You reach deep inside for the last ounce of patience you have stored away in a full proof tupperware container and force a smile.

"Okay, let me have a look." You bend to examine the toe as she rips off the grimy sock. Children gasp and you almost pass out from the smell. You clutch the desk for support while you inspect the torturous toe. You scan every inch but see nothing but a foot desperately in need of a good scrub.

"Honey, I think it'll be okay. Just try P.E. and if it hurts too much, just sit and watch."

"He always sits out, Teacher," the Smart Aleck adds.

The whiner sniffles and lays his head against your arm. Tears, drool and green ooze drips down your sleeve.

Then suddenly the Space Cadet walks over and pokes you on the arm.

"Hey, teacher, teacher, when are we going to do our program?"

WIMPS, BULLIES, AND BOSSY BUTTS

The wimps hide in the corner of the playground underneath the fort, lie on their stomachs and draw in the dirt.

"Come on, get out of there, you Scaredy Cats," the Bullies yell. One of the bullies jerks one of the wimps by his sleeve and drags him out.

Meanwhile the Bossy Butts tell everyone what to play, how to play, and who they can play with.

The wimps give the bullies their candy so they'll go away. The bullies kick the dirt, grunt and run away, proud of their feat. The Bossy Butts tell you when it's time to go in.

"Yes, it's time to go in," you think. The heat is sweltering and your patience is melting into puddles of distress. It's time to pack book bags and go home. And it's time to erase the board and try to take the type out of the stereo."

ERASING THE BOARD:
TAKING THE TYPE OUT OF THE STEREO

Just as you erase the chalkboard at the end of the day, try to erase the chalkboard in your mind. Your may feel like you're beating your brains together just as you beat the erasers together, but you have to get rid of some of the dust. If you tag and label and stereotype too much then the dust will clog your vision.

Let's face it, we don't want to stereotype kids or anyone else, but just as kids we naturally sorted our M&M's by color to eat them and peeled the Oreo apart and ate the creme in the middle first, we naturally lump kinds of people into groups or label them with tags. There are certain physical traits, character traits, certain patterns of behavior which do cause us to label or tag children, groups, and even adults. When you go to the movies, you instantly recognize the *dumb blonde,* the *hard nosed cop*, the *nerd*. Children and adults both learn to cope with situations, get attention and influence others around them by their actions, whether desirable or undesirable. A child may whine because he has learned it gets him attention or a child may throw tantrums because people give into him.

A teacher can't possibly change all learned behavior or personality traits but a teacher can look underneath, give guidance, accept children as individuals, and try to modify behaviors in the classroom. She can work with parents to reinforce appropriate behaviors. Even the stereotypical smart aleck or whiner will have a good point or two, so it is inherent that you, as a teacher find it. It may be the scavenger hunt of your life but the treasure will be worth more than gold, for you and the child.

So, when you find yourself settling into a recliner chair tilting backwards towards the floor and weighted down with children's faces that have lost their shape, names that all sound the same and personalities that have meshed into a lump, throw your foot forward, and stomp your foot down. It's time to get out of that chair and erase the board.

TIPS

- Look for at least one positive thing about each child. Remind yourself of it daily. If you need to, write it down and list the positive things the child does. Focus on it and praise the child for it. Look for positive situations or ways to incorporate that aspect of the child into the classroom activities so he or she gets attention for it. For instance if a child is very strong willed, but creative, be sure to incorporate art or science experiments into your plans so he or she has a time to feel successful and shine. Learn as much as you can about the child, his homelife, background, personal interests or sports so you can have a common thread to communicate with him and you will gain a better understanding of him in the process. If you discover he has a personal interest such as computers, swimming, etc., be sure to capitalize on it in class and in your personal relationship.

- Try to disassociate the behavior of the child with the child. Stress to the child that if you dislike or disapprove of a behavior, then it is the behavior you dislike, not the child.

- Never label or tag children in front of them, other children or other teachers. Avoid gossip in the teachers' lounge and avoid judging a child on past experiences or another teacher's comments. Different children mesh or clash with different teachers so a child that is a handful to some one else may be a pleasant challenge to you.

- Strive to help each child develop positive self esteem.

- If you have labeled or tagged a child in your mind, set written goals for you and the child so you don't pre judge and set false pre-expectations. You don't want to fall into the self fulfilling prophecy.

- Use behavior modification techniques to help guide and change inappropriate behaviors. Be specific to the child's actions and don't criticize the child's personality or demean the child. Include the child in a plan of action for behavior change. Give specific examples and set specific goals. Also set realistic goals. If a child has several problems, begin by focusing on one and work to change one at a time. Reinforce the child for changes in the behavior and for effort. For example; if the child whines constantly, set the whining as the behavior to be changed. Discuss with the child different types of voices to be used (use positive words such as *let's use a nicer voice, a softer voice, an inside voice*) set up rewards for efforts. Be consistent.

- Use positive reinforcement as much as possible.

- Discuss types of behaviors and dealing with problems in the classroom. Read stories that feature different characters and discuss the type of character: the bully, the class pet, etc.

- Use role reversal and role playing to act out situations, behaviors, reactions, etc. Discuss appropriate ways to handle situations.

- Have each child keep a journal and record positive things that happen. You can keep one journal for problems and perhaps another for positive comments. Encourage the child to see how many positive comments he can include. Make it a contest to see if he can enter more things in the positive part of his journal than the problem part. Reward him when he does.

- Remember that underneath the facade of the bully, the whiner, the smart aleck, and all the other stereotypes, there is a little person needing to be nurtured and loved and recognized and that is your special job. Behavior often times is a symptom of another problem so look for reasons behind the behavior. If you dig far enough, sometimes beneath layers of hard rocks and soil you'll find the root of a flower just waiting to burst through.

SPAGHETTI JUNCTION

You inhale sharply as you approach the mangled and twisted curves of a dozen roads forging together. On the one way street your instincts knew which way to go, but when you see spaghetti junction you panic. Much like your classroom, there are many roads to take. If you approach your class with the attitude that *my way is the only way*, you are headed down a one way street that will probably lead to a dead end. Adaptability, versatility, and flexibility should be the rocks at your inner core.

When you say *draw a picture of a house,* the different versions may range from the detailed replica drawing to a spattering of colors left open to interpretation. One child may hiss and spit and pound his fists at an activity only for you to discover it is out of frustration, not disrespect. One child may not bring in his homework, not because he is lazy, but because his parents are working two jobs to put food on the table and can't take him to the library to do his research. Another child may be extremely quiet, but on further notice you discover it isn't because he just wants to be good, but because he has a family problem at home he wants to hide.

Interpretation depends on which side of the glass you're looking into. So, before you pounce on one child and summarize a behavior, attitude, or performance on the obvious up front, dig deeper for other clues. Always listen before you leap. Sometimes your mind and the mind of a certain youngster may not be in sync, but if you take the time to listen and understand the child's point of view, you may discover the mind of a creative genius other than yourself or the turmoil of a child with problems that needs your guidance rather than your judgment.

The following is a letter written to a teacher from a parent. Credit is given to the author. Her words express so well the sentiment of individuality which teachers need to foster instead of throttle.

LETTER TO MY CHILD'S TEACHER

by Reba Bonnat

A Texas mother wrote this letter challenging educators to value the variations in children to the *Texas Outlook*, a publication of GAE's sister affiliate in Texas.

Dear Teacher,

Today I entrust to you one of my cherished blessings. She comes to you with shiny hair, patent shoes, a brand new dress and stars in her eyes.

There is only one general category into which she fits...girl. In all other things she is a variation from the mold.

For the first five years of her life, her father and I tried to let her be an individual. She does not know that conformity has been enshrined by some people.

There is an old proverb which says: If the shoe fits, wear it. Please don't make her wear it if it doesn't fit. You would not think of trying to squeeze her feet into the shoes of the girl across the aisle just because they are both five years old. Please don't try to fit her intellect, her emotions, or her personality into a mold of what a five year old should be.

She may hear a different drum beat. She may have different dreams and different fears. Sure she has to walk the wide road with the mass of men and women. But she may want to chase a few butterflies down side roads, and she may need to gather a few flowers on the way.

Yes, there will have to be rules, but be sure those rules contribute to her growth and that they are not only for your convenience.

If she doesn't learn to read and write when your lesson plans say that she should, do not consider yourself a failure. If she does, do not consider yourself a success.

A more accurate indicant will be those stars.

Can you keep those stars shining in her eyes?

CHAPTER 5
OH, LORD, WHY DID I EVER DO THIS?

Hacking coughs explode like time bombs through your room. A mixture of fever, gunky green slime dribbling down children's noses, and dissatisfied stomachs tears through your room like thunderstorms tear through trees.

"It's flu season already," you hear one of the teachers whisper in the faculty lounge, the dread in her voice sounds as if she is preparing for tornado season.

Your stomach tumbles like a washing machine on spin cycle but you fight off the nausea seeping in. You're not going to catch EVERYTHING the children get, you tell yourself.

You bend over a child's desk to help him with his work and just as you lay your hand on his desk, his lunch decides it isn't happy inside his stomach. Without any kind of warning he throws up, all over his book, his papers, his clothes, his desk and you. Your hand is covered, your blouse is spotted and your shoes are splattered. Your stomach rushes to your throat and you swallow, trying desperately to catch it before you join him in the clutches of the *lost lunch* crowd and have to fight for a cot in the school clinic.

Screams, squeals of disgust, giggles, and hints of morbid curiosity filter through your classroom.

"Ill.... look, he threw up."

"Look, it's all over him."

"Oh, gross!"

"I think I'm gonna barf, too!"

"P-u!"

Half of the class joins in a chorus of retching noises while the other half pinches their fingers together like clothespins to hold their noses. You pat the child on the back and order one of the children to go to the office for help, one to bring paper towels, and another to get you the trash can. You attempt to help him to the bathroom and exercise damage control at the same time.

The rancid odor penetrates your nostrils, your clothes and your classroom. The poor child is in tears, the class is in chaos, and you are wondering, "Oh, Lord, why did I ever do this?"

THE PROFESSOR NEVER SAID
THERE'D BE DAYS LIKE THIS!

Help finally dawdled in. A clean up crew and a para professional arrived on the scene just long enough for you to go to the restroom.

You quickly grab paper towels and scrub your arms and hands. You try to salvage your clothes from the surprise attack you just endured and try to wash all the germs down the drain. Maybe you should have purchased a plastic rain coat for your flu season wardrobe you think. You slurp down a quick coke in the lounge and a pack of crackers to settle your own tormented stomach. Then you check on the child in the lounge while the para professional takes your class outside for a few minutes to let your classroom air out.

The Principal pokes his head in the lounge and calls you into his office.

"I need to talk to you. It seems we have a little problem. One of your parents called and has complained."

Your eyes roll forward, bulging at the lids.

"What about?" you ask, trying not to let panic jolt you into hysteria.

"Well, I know there's nothing to this, but it seems the parent is upset because you had the children close their eyes and think of something to write a story about and then you asked them to draw to music. She thinks you're trying to hypnotize them or brainwash them."

A nervous giggle of shock escapes through your opened mouth.

"You're joking?" you ask, feeling the blood drain to your feet and numbness envelope your body.

"No, I'm afraid not. I think we should just sit down and have a conference and explain what you were doing."

"But the children were drawing while I played "Mary Poppins." And I just asked them to close their eyes to think of a place they'd like to go, just picture it in their head, and then draw it. It was a creative writing exercise, that's all."

"I understand," the Principal said, "now, don't get upset. I'll let you know when the parent is coming in."

You fight back the tears as you return to your class. You've devoted your life to teaching and nurturing children, and now somebody is questioning your intent. Your heart aches like bubble gum that's been chewed twice and your body feels like it's been torn into bits.

You walk back into class, pausing momentarily to regain your momentum. The smell of the room slaps you in the face and reminds you of the crisis at hand. The kids are bouncing off the walls. The para professional needs to return to her other duties and you are greeted with frowns from 29 children with their noses pinched tightly together and their eyes crossed.

"Can't we go somewhere else?" one of the children begs.

"Yeah, it stinks in here!" another complains.

"Yeah, it makes me wanna puke," another adds.

"Teacher, I don't feel good," a little girl whispers to you as she tugs at your still damp sleeve. Then she burst into tears.

You feel like a twice baked potato. You look at your plan book and then look at the clock. How many hours are there in one school day?

The Professor never said there would be days like this, you think, as you line up the class and move to the hall. But of course, your mother never told you about PMS, socks that evaporate in the dryer, or multiple orgasms either.

RUNNY NOSES, ITCHY HEADS
AND CHICKEN POX MANIA

You're fourteen boxes of kleenex away from setting a world record for the most number of kleenexes used by one class in a single month. There have to be statistics on it somewhere, and you're thinking of assigning it to your class as a research project except you have so many absent that you can't fit in your regular work much less a project. Great big globs of slimy gooky green junk dried on dirty faces greet you daily and if it continues you may apply to the Guiness Book of World Records.

Then one day you happen to notice a child sitting in the library corner clawing fiercely at his head. You shrug it off until an hour later you notice he's still clawing.

"He's got snow in his hair," a little girl whispers.

Better check this out, you decide. Yep, tiny little flakes are in his hair, but they aren't snow. In fact if you look close enough, you can see movement. Suddenly your body itches all over and you immediately call for your class to form a line. It's pow wow time with the school nurse.

You wait at the clinic door and one by one, heads are searched for any delightful traces of head lice. Word spreads through the class faster than the 6:00 news can report a natural disaster and soon each class is forced to take its turn for inspection.

"Send this note home," the Principal orders. It's the same note as last year's with only the date changed and there are no names to protect the innocent.

For the next few weeks paranoia possesses you like a demon and you find you can't help a child with his work without first exploring his head.

You've washed, shampooed and sanitized everything you own at least three times and you still itch.

Then one day you notice another child sitting in the library corner, once again clawing and scratching. You immediately search the child's head, but find nothing. Then he lifts his shirt and you see the tell tale signs of red bumpy blistery spots that are jumping across the child's stomach. Chicken Pox Mania has begun!

Another note goes home and you mark your calendar; Chicken Pox, Day 1. Immediately you count days of exposure, being contagious, and illness and figure between 29 kids in your room, this mania could last well beyond spring break. Scheduling the children's make up work, detecting new outbursts, and dealing with the return of scabby crusty bodies certainly takes the monotony out of your day.

Then one day you discover yourself clawing at your own stomach. You ignore the facts staring you in the face and resist the temptation to look, in the beginning. But finally, curiosity and itching dig at you and you have to lift your shirt. A shiver of recognition rivets down your spine as you note tiny red blisters popping out on you as fast as popcorn popping in the microwave. You instantly pick up the phone and dial.

"Hey, Mom, uh, listen, didn't I have chicken pox when I was little?"

Silence.

"No, oh. (silence) I just wondered."

Your eyes glaze over as you look into the mirror and watch the red spots bounce across your face. Through clenched teeth you claw at your back.

"Well, Mom," you sigh, "I guess you can finally put that one in the baby book."

THE CLASS FROM HELL

"Oh, so you're the teacher who is honored with the class from Hell," the other teachers smile and tease you.

You draw a puzzled breath. Why does everyone keep saying that? Do they know something you don't know? Have they stacked their classes with their favorites like coaches do in baseball and dumped all the derelicts in one room?

So, these kids have a few problems. They're still just sweet innocent children and you're trained to deal with these problems. You wanted to work with needy kids, to feel like you're making a difference. A challenge: that's how you look at it.

The class from hell, ha! They'll see.

If you teach middle or high school, you may find yourself cussed at, spit on, and wondering if your school has a warden instead of a principal. Smoking cigarettes becomes a minor issue as you have to deal with drugs, weapons in schools, teenage pregnancies, racial problems, gangs, and teenage suicide. Teaching your subject becomes second to the real life crisis that you catch wind of in the halls.

If you teach younger children, you set out a few simple centers for the kids the first day, plan a short story, simple art and games. In the first hour of the day the room is demolished and you've thrown your plan book in the trash can.

George has a mouth full of paste, Natasha is sticking crayons up her nose and Pauline is ripping the pages out of the storybook and trying to eat them. Joe is banging his head against the wall, Willie is throwing blocks at Doreen's face and Teresa is racing in circles on top of the table. You prop one into time out and then dive to catch another from jumping off the chair with six pairs of scissors in his hand.

By the end of the first week you've called your local child and family services department twice, discovered that one of your children was a *drug* baby, learned that one of your children has lived with at least seven different families, none of which he belongs to, and you've had to visit another child in an institution where his mother placed him for fear he would hurt the other children in the family. She's on welfare and has five children, each by a different father, none of which lives with her.

At the end of the first week you can no longer laugh when the others tease you about the class from Hell. You're living it. You've also climbed down off your pedestal because the challenge means really hard work. Each day your stress level peaks like egg whites beating into meringue. You feel like you're trying to dig your way to China with a toothpick and trudging into a never ending hole. Progress, if there is any, is slow and smattered in tiny rivets throughout the year. Yes, you may have the class from Hell but some of your students may be living in Hell, too, and although you know you can't change things forever, maybe you can make a tiny difference, at least for a while.

You decide to leave your nice gold chain at home for fear one of your kids will choke you with it. If only you could leave your heart. You massage your aching muscles as you crawl into bed after a fatiguing day, but nothing can massage your heart for it bleeds for each little child. Yes, you may have the class from hell. The challenge is hard and the pay off is little, but you know that tomorrow you'll get up, get dressed and do it all again.

TEACHERS: QUIRKS, PERKS, PASSIONS & PET PEEVES

Your pet peeve may be another teacher's passion. Your quirk may be the mark that will distinguish you in the minds of the youngsters you teach. And your passion for teaching may salvage a child distraught with the learning process.

Some teachers prefer science, others math. Some like to dance and sing while they teach and others like to excite learners with attention getting devices like props, hands on activities such as bringing in a real brain to view, or even magic tricks. Whatever your quirk or passion, be sure to utilize your uniqueness to grab the kids' attention and to interest them in learning.

These comments were taken from a survey of teachers' opinions:

Why I chose teaching as a profession:

To love handicapped children and all children. They have an unreachable innocence.

To follow my child through school.

After having several bad teachers who treated us very mean, I decided that I could do better and would treat children with respect.

I like to work with children.

A teacher made me feel good about myself and enjoy learning. I wanted to give something back to another child who might need that feeling.

Biggest Reward of Teaching

The smiles when a light bulb goes off, the hugs of thanks, and the days that they make me *smile*.

Watching a child that was struggling catch on to the problem.

Watching information finally sink in.

Seeing the children grow through what I teach them.

Knowing that I'm helping a child feel good about himself, learn and grow.

When children love you and you see them grow and love others around them.

When you helped some child with a problem.

Biggest Gripe of Teaching

Parents who expect me to raise their child and give no support.

Overprotected parents who think they know more about teaching.

Not being able to do things your own way, having too many rules to follow.

Paperwork, meetings, and red tape.

People in higher offices telling teachers how to teach when they themselves have never taught in a classroom.

Sweetest Thing a Child Ever Did

A child told me I was beautiful and that I sing well, which is not true.

A child told me I was a lot of fun.

A child enrolled me in the pin of the month club.

A child wrote me poems, letters, and cards.

A child asked if he could give me a hug.

A child asked me to come to dinner at his house.

A child offered me his stuffed animal when I wasn't feeling well.

A child offered to buy me an ice cream cone one day when I said I didn't have any money. He bought it for me anyway and surprised me with it.

Biggest Catastrophe in Your Class

I poured plaster of paris water down the sink and it hardened in the pipes.

I spilled gobs of paint which took hours to clean up.

A gerbil bit one of the children. She screamed for an hour. Then the next morning when we came in the mother gerbil had eaten the baby one.

We used soda and vinegar to make a volcano. There was too much of something and it exploded all over everything. It took days to find all the white spots.

A child who threw up all over a puzzle which had lots of pieces.

We cooked soup and the vegetables were hard when it was time to eat.

We did bubble painting but the mixture didn't work right and dripped all over the kids papers.

Pet Peeves

Nose pickers.

Children who come to school for a long period of time without having had a bath.

Things not put back in their place.

Calling my name 100 times when I don't look up immediately.

Tugging on my clothes, saying, *teacher, teacher* instead of using my name.

Interrupting.

Children making *farting* noises with their arms and armpits.

Favorite Teachers

My first grade teacher because she taught me to read.

A teacher that told stories and included the kids in the class in the story.

A junior high teacher who read *Where the Red Fern Grows* and cried the whole time. She taught with emotion and we loved that.

A teacher who began class the first day of class by ripping a phone book in half with her fingernail. That got our attention immediately. Then she had us do arm wrestling which taught me to respect her.

A teacher who used games to teach us.

My fourth grade teacher who took us on trips.

My kindergarten teacher because she was so sweet and hugged us everyday.

Worst Teacher

One of my teachers who ran the classroom like a prison. She allowed for no flexibility, no group work, no talking — nothing.

A teacher who accused my sister of cheating on a test. Even though my sister was a straight A student and did not cheat, the teacher humiliated her by screaming and yelling so loud you could hear her all the way down the hall. She also threatened to withhold her grades on her report card.

A teacher who used to slap our hands with a ruler if we misbehaved.

A sweet old man who was very nice, but had no control over the class. While he taught, the kids ran around the room, jumped on the desks and out the window. He got frustrated sometimes but just kept right on talking instead of stopping them.

A teacher who wasn't fair. She punished the whole class or table for what one child did.

A teacher who ripped kids' papers up if she didn't like their work or art.

CHAPTER 6

POUND THAT GAVEL:
ORDER IN THE COURT

When the honeymoon was over everyone changed into his or her play clothes to get comfortable. That's when you noticed a few changes in the children, not drastic but noticeable. Now it's mid year and either the trailer you're packed into is shrinking or everyone is getting fatter because the elbow room between students is zero.

With that growth in bodies and minds comes also the wondrous discovery of the multiple personalities within each child. As with recycling, teachers discovered multiple personality disorder long before psychologists even had a clue. Cold weather, rainy days, and the unpredictable changes in barometric pressure gives rise to the transformation of a once calm bunch of kids into one of bedlam. Rain in the air stimulates children's activity level as if they'd devoured candy bars for breakfast. No one wants to work, no one wants to share, and no one wants to listen. Their voices have been flipped to high volume and body parts disassociate from brain cells, taking on a mind of their own. Bodies fidget, wiggle, and move with seemingly no control by their owners.

Personalities clash, tempers flair, and the rules you established at the beginning of the year are like swinging bridges ready to be tested and rocked. So, before the bridge collapses and you find yourself swinging from a loose rope like a Tarzan groupie, pound that gavel and get some order in the court.

TIPS

- Set up rules in the beginning of the year. Reiterate occasionally and modify if needed. Keep rules simple and post the rules so they can be seen.

- This is definitely a time to include more hands on type activities for kids.

- Practice positive discipline; set up rules in a positive manner. Example: List rules in positive statements such as walk in school, run outside, use inside voices in the classroom, be prepared, respect other's life spaces. Try to avoid statements such as no running, no spitting, or general statements such as be good, be nice, etc. Also try to consolidate your list so that it isn't too lengthy. You can list specifics under general rules and be sure to clarify as specifically as possible.

- Be a good role model for behavior by using a quiet voice yourself. The louder you are, the louder they will be. Respect children, their space, and individuality.

- Be fair, firm and consistent.

- Praise and reward. Give each child a positive self concept. Never embarrass, humiliate or demean a child, especially in front of others, and don't be sarcastic.

- Set up a reward and consequence system if you need. You can do this in a variety of ways and can adapt to your class, their needs and interests. Set up a system to keep track of positive behaviors such as pockets with individual child's name on it. You can use a star chart, stickers, even paper strips, cards, or cars with a green light, yellow and red light on it. Do this on a daily basis. If a child misbehaves or breaks a rule, he has to pull a card. For example, he pulls his card from green to yellow as a warning. If he breaks another rule, he might have to go to time out. Always give a child a way to earn his way back with positive behavior or efforts. You can give rewards at the end of the day and also for a certain number of positive days. You may want to use paper animals such as bears for *bear hugs*; write the child's name on it as a reward or list his reward on it. Rewards can include free time, library or computer time, free homework pass, game or art time, sitting by the teacher, being a special helper, etc. Let each child know your expectations, rewards, and consequences. Include the class in a discussion of rules, rewards and consequences.

- Encourage each child to be responsible for himself, his work and behavior. While teams and groups can influence and help others, it's best to teach each child self discipline.

- Individualize. Set up personal contracts for behavior if necessary. Don't punish the whole class for one child's behavior.

- Organize leader and helper charts for the class.

- Use the time out method. Set a special place where the child can retreat to collect himself. Consequences can also include loss of outside time, redoing work, extra work, etc. Approach this method in a positive way, not as a punishment, stressing that the time out is to give the child time to think about his behavior and collect himself.

- If you plan incentives, do so in such a way that each child can feel successful and no child will be humiliated. Allow for individual differences. For instance, if one child is a fast reader and another a slow one, adapt your goals and rewards to suit the individual. Reinforce each child for efforts and progress at his or her own level.

- Have your plans individualized. Also remember that the children have grown in the middle of the year and may need more challenging work, more responsibility. Keep them busy but challenged. Challenged children who are stimulated by an exciting learning atmosphere present fewer problems. If you're having a problem with a child, study the reason and adapt to help the child, whether the child is ill, having family problems, bored, etc. Also, look at your teaching style and methods and see if you might need to alter your methods to include more hands on experience, visual aids, fun projects, etc.

- Weekly Reports can be helpful. Try to structure your report simply and in positive terms. Leave a space for comments. Phrase comments as positively as possible. Be specific. For example; nice work on your artwork, great job on your math test or next time think before you speak, watch your time in math, etc. Kids will remember the specific comments more and they will help their self concept.

- Leave kids notes in a jar or mailboxes. Use a Compliment box or jar. Use plain note paper or use cute notepads available from supply stores. Also write or list names of children on the board when they receive a compliment not just for ones who haven't finished work. Children can also do this for one another.

- For older children, adapt the rewards. You may need to use a citation method. For infractions of rules, children get a citation. After a set amount, the child has to stay for detention. Also set up positive rewards; a pizza party, movie, acting out a play, a walk and extra free time, homework passes, etc.

- When the different personalities emerge, try to remain calm. Reacting angrily to children may jolt you into a battle of wills with some children. You may have to be a little tougher and may need to stress and review rules, but stick to them. And whenever possible, make sure the kids have time to exercise and expend their energy, even if you jog or dance in place to a record. A brisk walk, exercises, even new types of projects or a different approach such as more hands on types of study can elevate interest in the classroom.

- In the midst of the winter blues, plan special days, outings projects and shows to help sustain interest.

- If you're having discipline problems, consider not only the individual child and his problems, but your teaching methods. Are you meeting the individual child's needs? Are you creating a positive atmosphere and attitude with stimulating activities to challenge children. Have you talked with the child and parent to gain insight into the individual child and his family? How can you make your classroom more fun while teaching the basic concepts you want to stress?

R-E-S-P-E-C-T: WILL YOU STILL RESPECT ME IN THE MORNING?

"But I want the kids to like me, not think I'm mean," you think as you pin your *I love teaching* pin to your denim jumper.

"To get respect you have to be mean," another voice battles with your first.

Which one do you listen to? Back and forth, back and forth, the voices scream in your ear. There has to be a happy medium, you think.

You remember back to some of your teachers, best and worst. One teacher was sweet and kind, but while he wrote long geometry problems on the board, the class danced across the desk, threw spitballs and climbed out the windows. Another teacher screamed and yelled and made your stomach rumble as if you were in the middle of a hell, fire and damnation sermon. And then another ripped children's papers up in front of the entire class and forced even the class clown into tears.

Which was your favorite teacher? Probably the one you learned the most from, probably the one you liked and respected. Maybe it was the butterball grandma type or the hunk P.E. teacher or maybe it was the teacher who you liked because she treated you the way you wanted to be treated, with respect. She had rules. She demanded work. She demanded respect. She piled you up with homework, but she also taught you many things. She was fair. She was constant and consistent, not sweet one minute and volatile the next. You could count on her. You knew the rules. You knew what to expect.

That's the happy medium you want. If you have respect for each child, then he or she will learn to respect others. While you don't want to frighten young children by being too strict at first, you can't let chaos get a grip. So, set your rules, and be fair, firm, matter of fact, and consistent, but flexible if you need. Once you've set your rules and your class realizes you'll stick by them, then you can let your hair down and have fun.

You may want to dress like a pioneer and have everyone make pioneer crafts to learn about history or you may want the entire class to dress as their favorite storybook character and share their favorite book one day. If you provide stimulating and fun ways of presenting information your children will be able to handle the unexpected and will learn to love school as well as you. Vary your teaching style often and offer lots of hands on experiences to make learning more fun and challenging. Even middle school age kids enjoy hands on experiences rather than boring lectures. Remember, challenged children, children excited about learning, don't create problems. Visual aids and special effects all grab our attention. As adults and children, especially in our TV oriented society, we need stimulation. Make learning as fun as possible. You know you even fall asleep during long speeches at meetings, so don't bore your kids into naptime.

TIPS

Respect the child and he will respect you. Treat him as a person, not as an object. That teacher you liked as a child may have corrected your mistakes, but she did it in a positive helpful way, not demeaning or humiliating. Learn not only to talk to children at their level but also to *listen*.

Rules: you must have them! Children need guidance and structure. Let children be a part in making the rules, also setting up rewards and consequences. Help them understand the reasons behind the rules.

Be specific about comments. Comment on positive and negative behavior but don't attack the child.

Be brief and matter of fact, not emotional. Forget the lengthy lectures as they will slide off deaf ears and crash on the floor. State your case, enforce the rule and then let it go. Give children an opportunity to earn their way back in good graces.

Don't make *never* or *always* statements such as *you never listen, you're always misbehaving*. Those comments are destructive and your goal is to change behavior, not destroy the child's ego.

Approach children with the problem, state it and make a plan. You'll earn their respect and they'll learn that you care.

Don't use sarcasm, it is negative and children sense and feel hostility when they recognize it.

And remember, always wear clean underwear in case you're in an accident and carry a dime, no, a quarter now, for a phone call in case of an emergency. Some things never change. Love and respect each child and he'll respect you, even in the morning.

TEACHER WORKDAYS:
MEETINGS OR MAINTENANCE?

You have a teacher workday! A holiday for the kids. Yeah, a break for you. Or is it crammed with so many meetings and maintenance chores that you feel like a puzzle that's just been dumped on the floor in a 1000 pieces?

Teacher workdays that are planned and scattered throughout your calendar are scheduled to give you a day to breathe, to catch up. Of course, some would argue that you only work until 4:30 each day so how could you get behind? Never mind the stress and exhaustion that accompany trying to teach and maintain control of twenty to thirty bodies all housed under your care for six to eight hours each day. Then you have bucketloads of paperwork, weekly reports and report cards, meetings, bulletin boards, and organizational and housekeeping chores to do plus in-service hours to take.

The *to do* list you've written includes everything from cleaning out the art cabinet to finding all the missing game pieces behind the cabinets to filling out IEP's and scheduling conferences. And wouldn't it be nice if you could steal a few minutes with the other teachers just to talk? Your *to do* list grows longer as you learn of the grade level meeting and assessment of new texts for the next year gets filed in the middle of the list. As your list gets longer, your day gets shorter and your teacher workday, your catch up and breathe day becomes a test to see if you can keep your stress level from skyrocketing.

A few tips and remedies should help keep your blood pressure steady and your mouth from exploding into language inappropriate for the walls of your classroom and meant only for those seedy novels that you read when you throw off your teacher clothes and sink into the solitude of a grown up chair. And although as with every other job when the bell rings and you have to pick up and start your second job at home, if you've crossed off even one thing on your list, you probably need to pat yourself on the back.

TIPS

- Set realistic goals (3-4 not 30!) or you'll set yourself up for failure. Remember there are only 24 hours in one day and there's only one of you so don't stretch yourself so far you feel like a worn out rubber band ready to pop.

- Count the number of workdays for the year and divide the tasks between them. Set aside a certain hour or half hour for cleaning out the cabinet or housekeeping. Block your hours on your calendar, for example; 9:00-10:00 clean art cabinet, 10:00-11:00 average grades. Check things off your list as you go so you can see your accomplishments.

- The day before your scheduled workday, prepare your lists and have supplies ready so you can get started right away. Prioritize your list and focus on accomplishing one thing at a time. Arrive a little early and get started so you can take a break to chat with other teachers when they arrive.

- Save things you can do at home for home. Laminate your games, then take home to cut out while you're relaxing in front of the tv. Use your school time for things you can't take home.

- Enlist your own children's help for organizing, cleaning out, cutting, etc. Offer your children pay or privileges for their help.

- Plan a special lunch with fellow teachers and work hard all morning, then kick back and enjoy the social time or set a meeting over lunch and discuss things as you eat.

HOMEWORK: IT'S BEEN A HARD DAY'S NIGHT AND I'VE BEEN WORKING LIKE A DOG

School is for school and home is for fun! That is only a myth for student and teacher.

"Teachers have it so easy," you've heard people say. "They only work from 8:00-4:00, what hours!" Obviously spoken from the mouth of someone who has never taught school or even closely known someone who is in the teaching field. Ignorance may be bliss but it is still ignorance.

Homework—not only for the kids but for you, the teacher, becomes as routine and never ending as replacing the toilet paper in your kid's bathroom at home.

Your morning pre-planning period and half hour (if you get one) is filled with meetings, paperwork, committees, phone calls, copying and preparing materials for class, dealing with unexpected problems at school such as discipline or illnesses, and a much needed potty break for you. So lesson plans, centers to make and papers to grade are stuffed into your bag stamped with the red apple bearing the message *Teachers are Beary Special* and carted home. It's been a hard day, and your days and nights become confused as your eight hour day extends into the wee hours of the morning.

Your easy *teacher hours* drift into midnight madness after you are forced to take a little time for dinner and to provide the taxi service to your own children and their activities. Then, of course, since you are the teacher and experienced, you get flogged with helping organize and orchestrate half of the events in their lives, both in school and outside, Brownie and Boy Scout troops, church and Sunday School activities, and you often become the neighborhood *Mom.* Carpool problems make your head spin and household duties beg for your attention. Laundry multiplies faster than guppies and you thrive on paper bag meals for survival.

Your summer calendar gets posted with new centers to make, organizing your files, making bulletin board materials, and taking classes to keep your certification up to date. You may also fill your summer with an extra job *just to make ends meet.* Although you remember that *money is no object,* you have quickly come to realize that without it your electricity may be turned off, cable will be disconnected (can't live without that TV!) and your own children may go without shoes and the much needed braces for which you'll be paying on until retirement. (You may even need two summer jobs to pay for the metal that will be snapped, glued and plastered in your children's mouths, the metal that according to the bill you receive should be made of gold.)

At bedtime you feel like a battered exhaust pipe and so may the kids you teach. Three kids fell asleep in your class to the point of snoring and you've heard at least twenty five different excuses in one week for not having homework done on time ranging from the fact that one child had an ingrown toe nail that throbbed so bad he had to soak it in hot water all evening, to the fact that one child's grandmother forced him to watch educational tv all week so he could learn something since he didn't seem to be learning anything at school

"School is for school and home work is for the birds!" the kids say. You want to agree but fitting your curriculum goals into the schedule of your day is like cramming toothpaste back into the tube. And preparing minds for the next year and for life requires the discipline of a little bit of homework.

So, even though it's been a hard day's night and you've been working like a dog, you can't have your bone until you've done your homework. Then finally you can relax and collapse into bed, that is if you aren't passed out from fatigue in your big arm chair already.

TIPS FOR THE TEACHER

- Set realistic goals for yourself. You can't possibly make 20 new centers a week. Aim for one or two and build up your supply gradually.

- Use a calendar and record goals and accomplishments—write in notes for things to do in advance, prepare ahead.

- Enlist your own children's (or a friend's) help in making games or centers. Pre teens and teens might enjoy helping you and you can offer a small fee for their work.

- Trade off privileges or reward children for their help.

- Grade as many papers as you can in class. Use your time wisely. Also, let children trade papers and learn to grade them. Assign one or two children as the *checker* for certain papers. Vary this to give all children a turn.

- Organize your time—use times like sitting at the Dr.'s office, in lines for picking up children from activities, etc., to make notes, read, catch up on grading papers, etc.

- Make lists.
- Shop (grocery shop) in larger quantities; this saves time of going out daily.
- Set up carpools.
- Save notes and ideas and file from year to year, weed out unwanted or extras as you go.
- Prepare materials for your next day before you leave each afternoon. You'll leave feeling less anxious about the next day and the next morning you won't be so harried (especially if your morning tends to fall apart with your own children.) Missing shoes, over sleeping, notes to fill out and sign, and forgotten homework in the morning can throw your whole day off.
- Set a certain time each day for your homework as well as your kids. This establishes a routine for you and gives you quiet time as they work also.
- Utilize the small moments or breaks during your day to organize for the next, for example, while the children read silently, cut paper for tomorrow's project, etc.

TIPS FOR TEACHERS AND STUDENTS

Kids need homework but also need time for fun, outdoor play, extra curricular activities, and just quiet relaxing activities. Children need some homework to help them establish a routine for study, develop study habits, and discipline. However, bombarding them with homework may boggle their minds, frustrate them to tears, force them to rush and not retain information, create negative feelings, and exhaust them to the point of falling asleep the next day in class.

Consider the age of the student, time factors, season, difficulty and length of the assignment, and assignments from other teachers. Giving fourth graders a 350 page book to read in five days plus homework each night in other areas while another teacher has assigned a major research project will only stress kids out and you'll be defeating your own purpose.

Teach children time management. Help them make an assignment note pad for recording assignments, learn how to budget their time for long assignments, and record their progress. Give them a chart for each day and let them fill in a time for homework daily to establish a habit, if they have no homework one day encourage them to still use that time for reading, working on upcoming projects, etc. When working on a long project, help them outline different times to work on it and how to set short term goals to reach the big goal.

Label all assignments in an assignment pad or on a calendar.

Help them make an assignment folder or homework folder to put papers in to carry back and forth from school to home.

Try to be consistent and schedule regular days for certain assignments. For example; Spelling test on Friday, Math test: Wednesday. Being consistent will help children remember to study.

Gear homework to the child's age and abilities and build up as the year progresses. For example; 1st-2nd grade; 15 minutes, 3rd-4th grade; 30 minutes.

Have children record the amount of time it takes to do homework for a week or two so you can gage the appropriate amount to assign and can see the differences in rate of work of each child.

Let parents know your expectations about homework and be sure your class knows. Allow a leeway time for forgetting, but set limits and consequences within reason. For example; one day late is fine, two days late and you count off five points, etc.

Reward children for completing homework on time and give children a chance, within limits, to make up missed work.

If a parent and child are having special difficulties with homework, refer (yourself) and parents to *Homework Without Tears* for more specific and detailed plans.

Make sure the homework you assign is of value to the child. Children know and resent busy work and so do parents. If a child can learn a new concept or practice by doing twelve problems instead of two hundred, opt for the twelve or at least a reasonable number in between. Homework should be done to practice and reinforce material already presented. Be sure children understand directions before they get home.

Make a homework collection box. Set up a self checking or partner checking system to help cut down on your own grading time.

If children are working in groups or projects, give them ample time in class for research and group work. It isn't realistic to expect them to meet as a group outside school. Parents' and children's busy schedules make this impossible. Also make certain that each individual in the group knows and completes his or her part in the project. When grading, try to give individual grades as well as a group grade so those children who really worked hard on the project are rewarded for their efforts.

CURRICULUM NIGHT: PACKING IN THE TIDBITS

The papers noting your words of wisdom are xeroxed, the folders are prepared with all the tidbits of information you think the parents need to know, the child sized chairs are lined up ready for adult bodies to try to squeeze into, and the lump in your throat feels like a hunk of brick hard jello that won't dissolve.

If it's your first curriculum night or your twenty-fourth, you may still feel that gnawing in your stomach until the evening or afternoon is concluded. The unexpected question or comment from a parent or an ill-willed attitude could throw you into the spin cycle and when the night is over you might feel like a crushed, smushed up roach bug instead of the ladybug you are. Just when you think you're prepared for everything and that you've heard it all, some one with the brains of a rock and the tactfulness of a vulture may descend on you with the unimaginable. You are a center stage for inspection by every adult face that stares up at you from the two feet high chairs. Is it that their twisted and distorted bodies are causing them pain or that they already disapprove of you? It's hard to tell from the solemn faces that peer at you.

Some of the parents greet you with warm smiles and volunteer their services from chaperoning to monitoring the water fountains while others sit with ankles crossed, hands clasped, lips pressed tightly together, and necks craned, awaiting judgment on you until after they have witnessed the spectacle, I mean, spectacular presentation you are about to give. When you smile, you see this group lean forward to note the space between your front two teeth and the rash exploding on your neck. You stammer and stutter and find yourself having to concentrate on moving your tongue out of the way of your teeth so you can speak.

Then, there may be that one parent who storms into your speech, interrupts with questions such as, "Why do you lean on your left side when you talk?" or "Can the children bring oreos to school for snacks?" or even "Do you use new age tactics to brainwash children?"

Then one parent corners you for a conference after your speech, and describes in detail how nonconforming his precious child can be, how they have a completely open minded household with no restrictions and hope that you'll do the same so their child can foster his own development. Another parent tells you his child has an IQ of 250 and wants to know how you plan to challenge him. Another starts a gripe session of how poor the education is in the country, and another tells you how his cat is smarter than his child.

And then there is always at least one parent who will relate you to how BORED his child is, that in the first two weeks of school his child has learned absolutely nothing new.

How can you make this memorable night go smoothly, or at least as smoothly as possible and what is it exactly those fifty-eight faces want from you?

Obviously, you can't give them a day by day description of the curriculum and your teaching plans. But you can ease those fluttering moments of panic that stab at both parents and children. Basically parents come to curriculum night for an overview of the curriculum and to soothe their anxious minds; to know that they are turning their child's future over to a dedicated, responsible, capable person, one who cares about children, knows how to relate to children, knows how to present information to children and to parents and knows how to organize a class to facilitate learning.

What do you, the teacher, want parents to know? First of all, that you can fill those shoes. You will be a major influence in each child's life for several hours each day for several months. How you spend that time, the attitude you reflect toward the child and toward school and learning will affect the child. You will not only teach curriculum but hopefully help the child work on a positive self concept, the most important goal a teacher should have. A child may learn 25,000 facts in social studies or math, forget them and never need them again, but his self concept will affect every aspect of his life. Your enthusiasm for learning, attitude towards children, and basic teaching style should be the prime focus for the evening.

Other major things you want the parents to know are your basic methods of discipline, communication between parent and teacher, rules, privileges and consequences, structure of grading, basic outline of the curriculum, and basic expectations in class and for homework. You can plan to send more detailed outlines of curriculum goals each month or each grading period.

TIPS

- Introduce yourself, your background, personal goals and education, family and your teaching philosophy. Be enthusiastic and smile. If you act like you love children and school, then parents will instantly relax.

- Assure parents they are welcome to visit and encourage parent volunteers to help in different areas. Keep communication open.

- Have handouts prepared with outlines for each area. This will help parents remember later what you briefly talk about during the meeting. It may also trigger questions parents may have about specific areas.

- Handouts should include: outline of general curriculum goals, list of supplemental reading materials, copy of weekly reports if you have one, grading system details, discipline techniques, special policies of the school, dress code, school handbook, etc.

- Explain your method of dealing with snacks, calendars, lunches and costs, homework, center charts, organization of the class, and conferences.

- Explain, post, or list class needs such as bookbags, supplies, craft items needed, t-shirt sales or PTA information.

- Display books (texts and supplemental materials used) and other materials for parents to view.

- Have a sign up sheet for volunteers, room mothers, party needs, field trips, and any specific need you may have; for example; computer mom, collector of coupons,crafts, story hour, work with individuals or small groups, etc.

- Have samples of children's work for parents to see. Display.

- Explain homework assignments, requirements, amount of parent involvement in projects expected, etc. If curriculum night falls after school starts, take a few pictures or slides and show to illustrate your class arrangement, organization, etc.

One parent may know what you mean when you talk about "centers" while another may not have a clue.

- If curriculum night coincided with a general parents or PTA meeting have parents meet in individual classes or with teachers for the curriculum part. Designate certain times to begin and end each session so parents won't linger too long.

- Open the floor to questions but tactfully tell parents in advance that you won't discuss individual children during this time but you will be happy to set up a conference time if they feel a need. Have a sign-up sheet available.

- If a parent seems frustrated or upset, try to explain and answer his questions as calmly and directly as you can. If the parent persists, seems upset by your reply, or continues to question you, suggest he or she set up a time to come in and talk with you privately to discuss the matter. You may also suggest an administrator or counselor be available. If the problem is a school matter, suggest or refer them to the administration for help.

- Approach parents by always welcoming them into your classroom, letting them know that you want to work as a team for the benefit of their child and explain that their feedback is always welcome.And last of all, relax and try to be personable. Place yourself in the parent's place. Sometimes when parents come to school for a meeting they feel like they're back in school themselves so try to keep that in mind. Then others feel like they need to guard their babies like lions guard their cubs, and somewhat rightfully so. So, keep an open mind, drink a bottle of Maalox if you have to and then smile, it's Curriculum night, and you're on.

THE WEEKLY REPORT:
SMILEY FACES OR FROWNS

Smiley faces or frowns on a daily basis can make you and the kids you teach feel like you're training mice though a maze. And depending on the make up of your class (monkeys or zebras or angels) you may choose to opt for a weekly report or choose to defer. Consider the age and level of your class and specific expectations so if you choose to use a weekly report, you can tailor it to your classroom needs. And always, always try to use positive phrases so that your weekly report reinforces the child's positive behavior and offers helpful suggestions and guidance instead of becoming of a vehicle to vent your displeasure for a child. Children like to see check marks for positive behavior and work instead of a negative check. A parent's gut reaction to a negative report is frustrating (you know if you have kids of your own how your stomach knots and diarreah erodes your body). As the professional, try to ease the slap in the face from a negative report by using a professional attitude and by adding positive suggestions.

Examples of weekly reports follow, but remember to tailor yours to your specific needs and to the behavior system (rules, rewards and consequences) that you have established in your classroom. Keep your report simple, but leave a space for comments for both you and the parent in case you need further communication, specific details, or sharing.

You may want to make a permanent folder or holder for weekly reports at the beginning of the year. Take a folder and decorate it with your theme and the child's name. Laminate the folder. Then paper clip your weekly report inside or staple a xerox copy of the report for the grading period, for example six copies for a six week grading period if that's what you use. By keeping all the reports on one page, parents can see the child's progress or lack of progress over the time period and will be prepared for problems or suggestions you may feel necessary to discuss at a conference. Parents react strongly when they walk into a first conference and learn that their child is failing or misbehaving and they have had no warning or comments in advance. This also alerts parents to problems, miscommunication or concerns that they may have so they can contact you.

EXAMPLE:

Mon. Tues. Wed. Thur. Fri.

Has positive attitude

Completes assignments in class

Is Prepared

Completes homework

Follows classroom rules

Subject area

COMMENTS:

SUGGESTIONS:

PLEASE WORK ON:

PARENT'S SIGNATURE

SHORT AND QUICK COMMENTS FOR THE MIND FUDDLED TIRED TEACHER TO USE ON THE WEEKLY REPORT

Stamps or short personal comments can boost a child's confidence into outer space.

Search your educational supply store or craft stores for fun and encouraging stamps for young kids.

Positive	*(Smiley faces drawn or decorated)*
Way to go!	*Nice Work!*
Great Job!	*AWESOME!*
Wonderful!	*Much Improved!*
Thanks for thinking!	*Thinking is hard work!*
Very much Improved!	*Whale of a Job!*

Very Good!   *Out of this world!*
Good for you!   *Super!*
Keep up the good work!   *Great progress!*
You can do it!   *Great!*
Good thinking!   *Good Work!*
Terrific!   *Much Better!*
Very creative!   *Excellent!*
Bright Idea!   *Super homework!*
Wonderful!   *Terrific!*
Wow!   *Competed!*
What a Brain!   *What an Imagination!*

Encouraging Comments:

Study harder!   *Think before you speak.*
Watch your time.   *Use inside voice.*
Sharing is caring.   *Taking turns is cool.*
Take care of yourself.   *Back to earth; day dream later.*
Listen more carefully.   *Please do over.*
Keep trying.   *Try again.*
Please fix.   *Neater please.*
Please follow directions.   *You need practice.*
Ask me for help.

COPING WITH CONFERENCES:
SURVIVING THE S'S AND U'S

You survived curriculum night with the help of Kaeopectate. Now the ordeal of meeting face to face with each parent in the parent teacher conference looms above you like dark clouds on a rainy Monday.

Juggling parent's schedules, trying to please, accommodate, and fit in twenty nine conferences in one day or a couple of afternoons is like squeezing into shoes two sizes too small. Having all the weekly reports, paperwork, samples of children's work, testing, and written suggestions for improvement compiled and ready may keep you up until dawn. Then the thought of sticking to twenty minute intervals with people you hardly ever get to talk to can make you want to hibernate at home with a cup of hot chocolate and your favorite *I Love Lucy* reruns.

S's an U's and all the other grades; they have to be explained. Fumbling for words and examples of work or behavior problems may give the parent the impression that you are a dingy ditz instead of a competent professional, so always be prepared. Unless the parent and his or her child are perfect in all ways, you will receive questions and sometimes be challenged.

Whether or not you think each conference will be an easy one or a tough one, you must always be prepared for the unexpected. Your expectations and the parent's may be light years apart. Some parents approach conferences with a wealth of knowledge about education and others don't have a clue so tailor your monologue and explanations to the middle ground.

What does the parent look for or expect? Information about his child's progress, samples of work to illustrate his level of achievement, projection for the future, suggestions for ways to help the child in school and at home, an understanding of the class set up, and whether said or unsaid, to know that you like his child.

What do you want out of the conference? To inform the parent of the child's progress, show samples of the child's work to illustrate his level of achievement, give suggestions for ways to help at home, to learn about the child's attitude towards school, and to learn more about the child and parent from the parent's point of view. Any feedback the parent can give you will be helpful in helping you to understand the child, his work and behavior in the classroom.

TIPS

First of all, be friendly, relaxed and professional. Try to put the parent at ease. Many parents come to conferences feeling intimidated, much like they did when they had to visit the principal's office when they were a child. Others come with lots of questions, stories to tell you about the child or themselves, home problems, their child's version of incidents in the classroom that you either don't know about or have a different version, or even complaints. To help you get a feel for the parent's attitude ahead of time, be sure to send a note home in advance (when you set up the conference) asking the parent to list any special concerns or questions they might have. This gives you an idea of problems that may arise and gives you advance warning and time to prepare your answer.

ALWAYS start out on a positive note. If you start off with a criticism, you'll alienate the parent immediately. Begin the conference with a friendly comment, then note a few positive things about the child. Only then should you tactfully, point to the problems or difficulties the child may have.

Set up your conference schedule in advance. State specifically your times but do try to be flexible and accommodating (within reason). No teacher should have to meet a parent at school at 11:00 at night for a conference. Stress to parents that the conference is an important time to discuss their child's progress, needs, and future so they need to make an effort to come.

List your conference schedule and let the parent know the time limit. Suggest that they let you know of any special problems in advance or if they feel they will need longer than the assigned time so you can set it up accordingly. Post your schedule on the outside of your door on conference day and try to stick with it as best you can. Have chairs sitting in the hall for the parents to wait in. On a table display some class books, drawings or projects for the parents to look at while they wait.

Be aware that the child in your class often acts differently in school than at home with his parent. You can listen and learn much from the parent. Pecking order, siblings, neighborhood friends, and reactions to parents and things at home will give you insight into the *whole* child. Then you can offer suggestions for help at home and at school.

Have sample papers, tests, report cards, progress reports, etc., prepared in advance so you can devote your attention to the parent.

Explain any tests, especially standardized ones you have given, their meanings and significance to the child, class, etc.

You and the parent may be loaded with various or different concerns and through talking be able to fill in missing holes of information about the child to help you learn more about the child. The parent may also come loaded with questions and a different version of events that have happened in the classroom. If you sense hostility or a longer time is needed to discuss things more specifically, suggest the parent come back and set up a longer conference, perhaps with the counselor available.

Talk about the individual child. Don't talk about other children, compare children in the class, or tell the parent how immature the entire class is. The parent isn't interested. They want to hear about their child.

Be as specific and concrete as possible. If there is a problem be able to cite specific examples. Have them written down.

Have a suggested plan of action ready for you and the parent. Be specific and focus on one or two problems that need to be worked on at a time, not several. Set realistic goals and a plan for rewards and consequences for the child.

Don't dominate the conversation. Ask the parent about the child's attitude, what he says about school, his likes, dislikes, etc. Ask the parent to share concerns.

Be sure to praise and cite positive things about each child. Even the ones who never get into trouble need to hear how proud you are so they'll keep up the good work. Remember to give the attention to those who try and praise efforts, too.

Try to look for the cause of a problem and discuss this with parents. Encourage parents to tell you if there are any problems at home, if the child or family undergoes any changes that might affect them; divorce, death of a loved one or even death of a pet, medications, illnesses (even minor), etc.

Don't be overzealous at the first of the year in your evaluation. Be honest and positive but don't make predictions such as, *your child should definitely be at the top of the class and move up next year.* A lot can happen in a year and children change and grow constantly. Evaluate the child's work up to a point, be optimistic, but leave the door open for unexpected changes and surprises.

You may choose to do all your easy conferences first as they may go faster. You may want to do all the difficult ones first and get them over with or you my want to intersperse them for breaks. It's a personal choice.

If you sense a hostile parent ahead of time, alert the counselor, principal, or your director and have them come to the conference or be available on standby.

Never degrade or criticize the child's person, especially in front of the parent. Comment on specific behavior, not the child or his personality. Be professional and specific. Let the parent know that you want to work as a team to help the child, that you both want what's best for the child. Do listen and factor into your classroom information a parent offers about a child's specific problems or needs which might make it difficult or unreasonable for him to follow certain rules in your classroom. For example, if you learn that one child has a physical problem with his knee, you wouldn't expect him to sit Indian style for very long or if a child has a fear of closed in places, you might let him leave the bathroom door slightly cracked.

Conclude the conference with a summary and your plan of action. Let the parents know when the next conference will be and that you are available to discuss the child at any time if the need arises. End on a positive note.

DIFFUSING DISGRUNTLED PARENTS:
YOU CAN'T PLEASE 'EM ALL

When you moved that tassel on your graduation cap to the other side and snapped that diploma in your hand, you knew you were ready for the classroom. Your gracious smile would entice every child and every parent within a hundred mile radius of your school and parents would make certain their children were on waiting lists for your classroom.

Then to your surprise, the day after registration, a couple of parents asked for their children to be transferred to another class. Their reasons: you looked too young, you weren't experienced, your earrings were too wild, your name was weird, or any of a thousand unexplained reasons. So don't be offended or become depressed if you discover that your chemistry doesn't automatically mesh with every parent or child you meet.

At the first conference you are approached by an angry parent who accuses you of not liking his child. Another insists you are teaching witchcraft because you read a fairy tale that told of magic. One parents begs you to discipline his child, another begs you not to.

Any and every conceivable grievance known to mankind or other forms of life not yet discovered will confront you and usually when you're having PMS, a bad hair day, or you've just eaten the mystery pork choppette dish from the lunchroom cafeteria and swallowed the eraser that one of your kids tucked inside.

Disgruntled parents will inevitably storm into your peaceful existence and knock you right off your teacher shoes. They are like those mismatched socks that seem to get eaten by the dryer. You never know when or where one of them might turn up. So, how can you avoid confrontations and disgruntled parents or can you?

First of all, accept the hard cold fact that no matter how hard you try and how open, friendly, organized, stimulating, professional, loving, enticing and dedicated you are, you just can't please them all. Psychotherapy may work to help cure the co dependent in you but over a period of several years of teaching, at some point, and at some time, you'll make someone unhappy.

How do you prepare for this reality, other than drawing your own blood, so that your ego doesn't sink like a rock in quicksand and what do you do when it happens? Practice a few techniques to diffuse the hostility and approach the situation professionally, then go home and let Calgon take you away.

TIPS

Accept the fact that at some point it may happen and try not to take it personally.

Try to remain calm. Keep an open mind and try to be objective.

First of all, try not to react. Your hands and stomach may have an attack of the shakes and your temper may flare like the hot smoltering breath from a dragon, but try to use a low, calm tone of voice and tell the parent that you want to sit down and discuss the situation or problem. Tell the parent you want to listen and then the two of you can work it out. Try not to get upset or defensive. This may trigger further emotions from the parent, and the situation may get out of hand and lead to a tug of war of emotions. Suggest the school counselor, principal or another staff member be present.

Try to understand the parent's point of view and the child's. Try to keep in mind that the parent is there because he is ultimately concerned about the child and the situation or problem, even if his ideas aren't based on truth, fact or reasonable information. A defensive parent may have had a teacher who he disliked or who disliked him and the parent may come into your classroom carrying his own insecurities. Or the child's version of events may be altered to attract attention, illicit sympathy from the parent or sincerely be a misunderstanding. The entire situation may be a total misunderstanding that you can clarify, so try to be optimistic and diplomatic.

Use *reflective listening*. Take a deep breath and calmly repeat back what you think the parent is upset about or the nature of the problem. Listen to the parent without interrupting and let him get his feelings out in the open. Make written or mental notes on points you need to address. Try to get the whole story; what the child may have said, another person, etc. Sometimes the version a child tells his parent is much different than the real version. Then other times his viewpoint may reflect inner feelings or part of his personality that you aren't yet sensitive to. It may tell you things you are unaware of, things the child experienced but didn't tell you, involvement of others, etc. You may be able to pinpoint a lack of communication, a miscommunication, an understanding of a deeper problem of the child or parent, and this may be able to direct you to a better understanding of exactly what the problem is.

Approach the parent as a professional, concerned teacher that cares about each child, his attitude, problems and one who cares about the parent. Stress that you want to work with the parent to clear the problem up. If necessary, suggest the child come in and you all talk together. Sometimes a parent can understand and help a situation by watching how the teacher and child react to one another and the teacher can do the same by watching how the child and parent interact.

Approach the parent with calm understanding statements to diffuse anger and help you both be able to discuss the problem. Suggestions are: *I hear you're upset about this situation. Tell me exactly what you have heard or what your child told you. I'm sorry you feel that way or your child does, but perhaps we can clear this up if we talk about it. We both want what's best for the child.*

Once the parent has had a chance to vent his feelings, explain your version, your rules, your reasoning behind whatever happened. Approach it from your classroom philosophy and explain that the rules are in the best interest of the child. If the parent is still upset, discuss further or try to include a counselor or other staff member to help better explain. Comments such as the following may help: *I'm sorry you had that impression. I like all of the children. If I discipline a child, I'm trying to change behavior and I try to stress to the child that I can dislike the behavior but still like the child. I'm trying to teach each child to be responsible for his own behavior and actions. We both want that, I'm sure.* Be sure to emphasize and credit the child with some positive comments.

Have a pre prepared signal to another co worker as a distress signal in case you need a counselor, principal, or other professional to join you.

Make a list or plan together with the parent to correct or improve the problem. Make a written plan. Be specific.

Remember to treat the parent with respect and stay friendly and calm. Fist fights and name calling may come natural, but they are as unproductive as a plugged up toilet. How you treat the parent will be a reflection and an indication to him of how you treat the child. And that's the impression that really counts.

JUST FOR FUN: COMMON REASONS PARENTS MAY PULL THEIR CHILD OUT OF YOUR CLASSROOM OR JUST MAY NOT LIKE YOU

Your eyes are set too far apart and you look mean.

Your eyes are crossed and they can't tell who you're looking at.

Your eyes are not the color they like.

You remind them of one of their teachers when they were young, one they didn't like.

You look too young.

You look too old.

Your voice is too soft and sweet.

Your voice is too harsh.

Your bottom is too wide.

Your nose is too long.

You forgot to smile 739 times while they were in the room.

Your room is too bare and not exciting.

Your room is too junky.

Their child wanted Mrs. So and So.

You look inexperienced.

You look like you're probably ready for burnout.

Your writing is weird.

You have a wart on your chin.

You dress too funny.

Your make up makes you look like a hooker.

You have an accent different from their own.

You've never had children so you couldn't possibly understand them.

Your fingernail polish is too bright.

You just don't look like you'd be a good teacher.

Your name is too hard to pronounce.

You have a reputation as being a *mean* teacher.

You were seen buying beer at a local grocery store.

AND MY FAVORITE:

You just don't look like you'd be good for my boy (or girl).

BREAKING THE MONOTONY

Your face may be blemish free and model perfect and your voice may clamor like music, but sometimes your class needs more than the viewpoint which comes attached to your persona to keep them challenged, entertained, varied and awake.

Storytelling

- Use storytelling to add interest, humor, and excitement to normal lessons.

- Make up your own stories from past experiences and about things that happen in class. Use children in your class as characters to personalize them.

- Encourage kids to tell their own stories. Practice the stories and work with them on storytelling techniques.

- Use story starters for creative writing; give examples or offer story starters. Examples of story starters: a sentence or first line which the child finishes, such as "When I opened my lunchbox there was a _____ inside," "My favorite food is _____," "The weirdest vacation I ever went on was when I _____." Other types of story starters are objects, pictures of books such as a stuffed animal, a picnic basket, a pair of shoes, etc.

Storytelling Techniques

- Introduce your story with a question, phrase, or with background information.

- Know your story.

- Practice telling the story by yourself, in front of a mirror, to a tape recorder, or to someone else.

- Add visuals such as props, a puppet, object from the story, poster, etc.

- Study your story and choose action and movements to accompany it. Imitate emotions and facial expressions, animal sounds, and other sounds in your story.

- Practice and use different voices for different characters.

- Vary the inflection and tone of your voice.

- Pace your story as well as the speed of your voice, slowing down or speeding up to add suspense or show action. Pause to add emphasis, increase tension, and give the reader a breather to assimilate the story.

- Encourage children's participation by encouraging them to add voices, act out character's actions, movements or actions.

- End your story properly; tie up loose ends and let the children know the story is finished.

Hands On Experiences

Children and adults bore easily when subjected to tiresome long lectures. Children especially learn better with hands on types of experiences. Incorporate as many different types of methods of teaching into your day to keep children stimulated.

Examples:

- Bring in models of replicas of things to study.

- Tour places to view how things are made, created, etc.

- Bring in items or have children bring in items that relate to your topic. For example, if you are studying fruit, bring in a variety of kinds of fruit, visit a market and buy some. If you are studying machines visit different kinds of factories or businesses and discuss the machines they use. If you are studying a foreign country, bring in items from that country, such as money, clothing, jewelry, etc., and prepare foods from that country.

- Use manipulatives to teach math, such as a variety of different types of counters, beans, buttons, candies, etc., as well as blocks.

- Have guest speakers bring in items to share, such as tools of their trade.

GAMES FOR LEARNING

Make learning fun by creating your own version of common games to teach children basic concepts. Here are a few basic examples, but feel free to use your imagination and think of your own.

Bingo: Make bingo cards to teach spelling, vocabulary, math, etc. Use a variety of kinds of counters such as M&M's, Skittles, jelly beans, seeds, etc.

Hopscotch: Play indoors or outdoors. Place numbers, letters, words, math facts in the squares and play hopscotch.

Baseball: Play an indoor version by setting chairs up as bases. Children divide up in teams and each child is asked a question (math fact, geography question, etc.). When the child answers correctly, he advances a base. If he misses the answer he is out. Three strikes and the team is out.

Bean Bag Toss or Ball Toss: The ball is tossed to a child and they must answer the question or name the word, etc.

Lotto Games: Make your own lotto games to teach words, facts, letters, numbers, picture recognition, etc.

Centers

Children of all ages enjoy choosing their activities for the day. For reinforcement of basic concepts, use a center approach. Learning centers are fun, stimulating, and provide more hands on experiences for kids. They can be done in groups or individually and you can organize them to meet the needs of your class.

- Children can choose centers when finished with seat work or in lieu of seatwork depending on the set up of your class. The centers can be store bought or teacher made and provide a stimulating way of teaching.

- You can provide some centers to reinforce curriculum concepts, some which are required, and some which are free fun centers. Fun free centers might include an art center, storytelling center, library and listening center, creative writing center, computer center, games and manipulatives center, and for young children, housekeeping and blocks areas.

- Choose a way to keep track of who has done each center and record the child's success or difficulty with the center. Some centers can be self-checking, some can be worked in partners or groups. Keep a list at the center for children to mark off when they have completed the center. When choosing the center, organize your system so children can choose centers but also set it up so that each child gets a chance to do each center. You may have a limit on the number of kids at a center so when the center is filled, you simply say that center is closed and the child chooses something else.

- Use a color wheel to designate the rotation of centers or use individual strips of paper for each child and each center to be placed in library pockets to visually show what center each child has chosen.

Bulletin Boards

- Use bulletin boards to enhance your themes and curriculum.

- Use bulletin boards to display children's work and art work.

- Let children help create your bulletin boards by using their art work, classwork, and assistance in planning the board. They may bring in items or pictures of relevance to place on the board.

- Make your bulletin board educational and use it as a teaching aid by displaying materials, objects or pictures relating to your topic of study or by making it into a concept or game board. For example, if you are studying fractions, display several parts of objects and have cards with the amounts printed on them. Children can place the cards by the appropriate parts.

FIELD TRIPS, GUESTS AND SPECIAL DAYS:

Exposure to guest speakers, taking field trips, and including special days and activities in your calendar can stimulate learning, make learning fun and enhance the curriculum you are working so hard to hammer into those heads. The world in itself is full of education and exposing children to all avenues of learning via the real world opens not only doors for expanding your curriculum but doors for expanding their minds. Helping children learn to adapt school knowledge to the real world and see its purpose gives them a reason to want to learn and will hopefully give them a thirst for more knowledge. It can also be fun for you and them or it can be a major headache that makes you reach for that economy size of Excedrin you hid in your tote bag.

Field trips and other special activities can help children form friendships and help them relax and see another side of you, but it can also enlighten you to hidden personalities and quirks of each child. The change in atmosphere or monotony sometimes causes otherwise obedient minds to question authority and try to stretch limits like rubber bands.

Take steps to prepare the children and yourself for any variation of your classroom day. Skip that part and disasters may turn your special event into a miserable experience and you may toss your teacher files into the trash and quickly search for an easier job such as driving an 18 wheeler.

Of course if your field trip involves a sleep over with thirty kindergarten kids or middle schoolers at a local zoo, you may opt to choose the trucking job first before you even venture on the field trip.

What can you do to make your guests, trips, and special days more successful? Planning is everything.

TIPS

GUESTS

- Plan guests to fit in with your curriculum, a unit, concept, etc.

- Give children background information on the guest first.

- Help children prepare a list of questions to ask the guests, write down the questions. Discuss and practice asking questions vs. storytelling (this helps storytelling from the children, for example; I lost my tooth, my grandma has no teeth, etc.)

- Prepare a follow up activity after the guest leaves, also write a thank you as a class or individually and mail to the guests.

- Discuss rules and behavior expectations before the guests arrive. Talk about appropriate responses such as clapping, laughing, raising your hand, participation, etc.

- Prepare your guests for the age level of the class, a time limit, and a brief outline or a few suggestions of what you want them to talk about or do with the class. Also take into account children with special needs and prepare your guests for them.

FIELD TRIPS

- Plan well in advance, make reservations, and check with the place a few days before your trip to confirm. Disasters happen if you aren't well planned. Children may be inconsolable if you arrive at a destination and discover that you weren't expected until the following week.

- Call the place and find out what specifically they offer; activities, guided or not guided, provisions, place for snacks, bathroom facilities, etc.

- If possible, try to plan your trip to coordinate with the curriculum so it will be more meaningful to the children. A trip to a log cabin will be meaningful and more relevant if you're studying colonial times, but not as interesting if you've been studying outer space.

- Prepare kids for the field trip by explaining the schedule, rules, procedures for grouping, activities of the trip, etc.

- Make and wear name tags, school shirts. Take a class roll. Discuss a plan so the child understands what to do if he or she gets lost. Have medical emergency release slips and permission slips with you at all times. Set up a buddy system.

- Plan snacks and foods, extra drinks, etc. Label.

- Plan and take an adequate number of chaperones or adults. Assign them a small group of children to supervise.

- If staying overnight, provide parents and children with a packing list. Keep items to a minimum.

- Have emergency medial provisions available and provisions for sick children.

- If you have a handicapped child, call and make arrangements in advance for special accommodations; front row seats for visually impaired, ramps for wheel chairs, etc.

- Discuss in advance what each child should learn from the field trip. Give an outline or list of things to look for.

- Give children a journal or note pad for them to write in about the trip.

- Summarize what you learned from the trip when you return. Write a class story or list information. Let children write stories, draw about their favorite parts. Make a class mural.

- Discuss expected behavior, rewards and consequences before the trip. Follow through.

- Compliment the children on appropriate behavior when you return.

- Take a large tote bag with wipes; band-aids, kleenexes, etc.

- When planning field trips, let older children offer suggestions, help plan.

- Give as much freedom as possible on the trip and try to relax and let the children enjoy it.

- Once you've counted the heads on the way and the way home, relax and enjoy the trip. You'll be twice as exhausted as a regular day, but you and your class will have a comradeship unlike that you've known before and the child who doesn't recognize you in the grocery store or at the mall, may just see you not only as a teacher, but as a person and perhaps as a friend.

SPECIAL DAYS

Special days can include anything from *Pretty Pajama Day* in Kindergarten when everyone wears pajamas, makes pizza, brings pillows and watches *Pinnochio*, to cooking German foods in 7th grade German classes. Any age student enjoys a *fun* day and remembers twice as much from the hands on experience as he does from dozens of mind boggling and boring lectures. Use your creativity and imagination to create special days for fun and learning that fit into your curriculum.

For special days, plan in advance and let the children understand the expectations. Enlist the help of parents to assist if you need. Let each child contribute needed items and help plan, then record by writing or drawing about the day.

SUGGESTED SPECIAL DAYS:

Preschool—Elementary:
Wee Willie Winkie Day
Bear Day
Storybook Dress Up Day
Gingerbread Day
Bubble Day
Career Dress Up
Circus Day

Rodeo or Western Day

Watermelon Day

Beach Day

Pilgrim and Indian Day

Crazy Costume Day

Backwards Day

Bike Day

Camp Out Day

Dinosaur Day

Fall Festival Day

Feast Day

Game Day

Oldies Day

Pirate Day

Stargazing and Space Day

Grandparents Day

Flag Day

Pioneer Day

Earth Day

President's Day

Field Days or Olympics

International Day

Travel: any state or country: France, Japan, Hawaii, etc.

Color Days

Letter Days: Example; Funny Feet and Freckle Face Friday, Wacky Wash Wednesday, Terrific Turtle Tuesday, etc.

Additional Suggestions:

Prepare special snacks or foods and art projects to enhance your themes.

For example, when studying a culture, prepare foods originating in the culture, when studying the alphabet, prepare a food and do an art activity for each letter of the alphabet. For example, for the letter "A" make applesauce, paint ants.

If you are studying plants bring in different types of plants for the children to see.

Children learn much more through the aid of visual stimuli and hands on experiences.

CHAPERONING:
WHEN GROWNUPS HAVE COOTIES

Chaperoning, one of those little extra tasks that come with the territory of middle and high school teachers, can turn you into your mother faster than you want to imagine. Chaperoning is that task of trying to regulate, watch, control and limit bodies that are almost your size or larger and who are at that age where they view you, the grown up, as having cooties. Chaperones may cause you to tap into your inner brain to keep one step ahead and make you vow that it is a torture worse than meeting the dentist drill at 6:00 a.m. on a Sunday morning.

While most functions will only require your presence to scan the dance floor for inappropriate attire and heavy necking, there are the restrooms, the halls, the outdoors and any and all crevices of the school to explore for wandering and devilish youngsters. As time accumulates into more centuries, so moral and social issues accumulate into more avenues of exploration. The spiked punch, the funny cigarette floating around, the huddles in the bathroom, weird stickers and various sniffing items, condoms, homosexuals, the football players ready to fight over one of the cheerleaders, the geek parade pulling another prank, the new formed gang, or the citing of a weapon force you to creep into the policing role of parenting and teaching.

"What do middle schoolers do at a dance?" one of the parents ask you.

You laugh. "Well, the 6th graders just stand around and talk and eat, the boys on one side and the girls on the other like a bunch of old married people. They rarely dance. Sometimes the 8th graders dance a little. Then the chaperones stand to one side, keeping a watchful eye on everyone and feeling as ancient as the dinosaurs."

Social functions are for you less controlled than your classroom. This has both its positive and its negative sides. You have the opportunity to observe the behavior and interactions of the students and inevitably gain insight into each student. If they see that no one is watching, they may even dare the risk of cooties and talk to you in a more friendly and informal way. You get a chance to actually see the M&M under the coating of each glowing child. Then you may also find yourself placed in compromising and unpleasant discipline areas such as drugs, alcohol and sex issues. Unfortunately, you can't crawl in a corner like a spider and spin your own web, ignoring them. You're there for guidance and that you must give, pleasant or not, so, give it in an understanding and professional manner. While you may feel like you are your own parent, if you hear yourself shouting *This hurts me more than it hurts you*, remember to try and place yourselves in their shoes. Try to understand the peer pressure and conflicts of each age and gear those questioning eyes and minds in the right direction. The children, despite their ambivalence for rules and seeming dislike for you, are somewhere deep inside begging you for help and hoping you will be there to keep them in line.

CHANGING TIMES: ROLL WITH IT BABY

"Teacher, we found a condom on the playground," one of your students yells across the playground as she points to the grass near the fence.

Your eyes explode from your head like balls from a pop gun and almost fall on your feet. You hurriedly try to grab them and poke them back in your head when you feel your ears switch into overload.

"Teacher, look, it's been used!"

"OOh, yuk!" another girl screams as a crowd gathers to inspect the treasure.

"Do you know what a condom is?" you find yourself asking, praying of course, that the answer will be no.

"Well, of course, teacher, don't you?" one of the girls asks. She rolls her eyes and flips you a condescending look.

Shock simmers through your body like a computer virus. The times have really changed, you think. When you were a kid the worst infringement you could imagine was to smoke a cigarette or get caught cheating on a test, or the unthinkable; flip someone *the finger*. You learned about sex in 7th grade, not 3rd, and you still believed in Santa Claus when you were 11.

Now epidemic proportions of major life crisis and issue problems plague schools and seem to be filtering down to younger and younger grades. Drugs, violence, sex, rape, child abuse, suicides, Aids, weapons in schools, even murders; where does it end and where does it begin?

Arguments over who is responsible for teaching children values range from passing the buck to parents, churches, and to you, the teacher. The breakdown of the family, morals and value systems has disintegrated like the slow evolution of land forms. The drive through window has become a way of life and music, tv and videos have turned entertainment into science fiction horrors that seem a natural part of everyday life.

Activists, clubs and support groups exist for all facets of our present day culture and solving the problems covering our globe seems impossible. You can't pinpoint the source behind the deterioration of values, because so many factors interplay into our lives. Churches, parents and teachers, all should serve as a model for the children of the world and should work together. As a teacher, you can't fix it for everyone but you can't ignore your part either. Unfortunately, facing the different and varying beliefs, viewpoints, and value systems of different families you teach can prove to be more difficult than a major international business merger.

So, what can you do? Call in the Swat Team? Hardly. Pretend you're still in the 50's; dream on! Although times change, people and children's basic needs stay the same. Focus on those basic needs. Circumstances, problems, and decisions require your understanding, patience, and guidance and as Steve Windward says, sometimes you just have to *roll with it baby.*

WHAT YOU CAN DO

Although you do have to roll with it sometimes, you also have to have strength in your convictions both as a parent and teacher. Just because some kids do drugs, listen to vulgar music, have sex at 12 or use profanity as their first language, etc., doesn't mean you have to accept it, condone it, or allow it in your class or home. Decide what your values and rules are and stick by them. Your class or family will respect you for your strength and they will learn from you about not giving in to peer pressure.

For several hours a day, you are a major role model for the kids in your class. Use this to positively influence the children. Take any opportunity (seize the moment) to discuss appropriate values and choices. Try to relate your curriculum and studies to the *real world* to help children see the meaning. Encourage guest speakers who have dealt with problems or have become *success* stories to come in and speak to classes. Involve the school in community service projects to teach values and ways to reach out and help others.

Offer your listening ear for any problem kids may have. Try to teach them problem solving skills and how to make choices, to believe in themselves, to stand on their own beliefs and not to give in to peer pressure.

The respect and attitude you have towards individuals, acceptance of their differences, and methods you use to deal with problems will serve as an excellent role model.

You may not think you are making a difference. You may not see it immediately. You may never even know you did it. But perhaps, years from now, if even one child remembers values from you and incorporates them into his life, you will have been a success.

Don't preach. It will instantly fall to deaf shoulders and may turn kids off. Use stories, situations, role playing, literature, books and movies, examples, and discussions to make your points.

Treat your class like a family. Treat them with respect and kindness. Have class meetings to discuss problems.

Listen to the kids when they talk, especially if they are confiding in you with a problem. Use *reflective listening*.

Become active and discuss problems with other teachers and school counselors who can offer you helpful suggestions. Encourage parents to work with you as a team and keep lines of communication open.

If your school doesn't already provide this, set up parenting classes, drug awareness programs, a counselor, etc.

When faced with a difficult problem, try to learn all about the *cause* and seek help for the child and parent.

Set up a "Problem Box" so children can seek help anonymously. They may write down their problem, place it in an envelope in the box. You may read the problem, write suggestions or comments on paper and place back in the envelope. The child can keep his identity and problem confidential while seeking help.

Last but Not Least:

Try not to watch the 11:00 news at night. You will not only develop agoraphobia but you may never sleep at night again.

CHAPTER 7
ANOTHER MANIC MONDAY

"Another Manic Monday
wish it were Sunday,
that's my fun day!"

The alarm roars at 6:15 and you fantasize that you smash it into bits on the floor and disappear under the covers until you hear that snow has fallen in southern Florida.

Exhaustion possesses you like a demon and your Friday party night has become a time for slouching on the couch, eating home delivered pizza and rolling yourself into the bed at 9:00 p.m. On Saturday you try to cram in errands, shopping, your children's ball games, cleaning, hair appointments, and all the various asundry things you can't fit into your work week. Sunday is filled with church, finishing up plans for the upcoming week, family time, and perhaps a few minutes of peace, relaxation or even *fun time*.

Just a few more weeks, you tell yourself, just a few more weeks until the holidays. The kids are already starting to get antsy and your *to do* list is longer than *Gone With the Wind*.

You dab powder over the dark circles waving at you underneath your bloodshot eyes and pluck the new gray hair out of your head.

Just a few more weeks until you can get a break. Halloween—pumpkins, cats, candy. Thanksgiving; turkeys, Indians, crafts, Pilgrims. Christmas—the program, decorations, home made gifts. Your plan book is exploding with too many ideas and the time to complete them all is shriveling away. You take a deep breath and try relaxation exercises as you step on the scales and hold your breath. You've got to hold off those five pounds because you know that holidays will destroy your diet. Only a few more weeks, you remind yourself, and you'll get a break. Now if you can only get through the holiday havoc.

HOLIDAY HAVOC

Halloween costumes and worse, the weeks of wired kids feasting on hordes of left over candy force you to rely on the hidden reserve of patience you have wisely stored away in the deep freeze.

Then turkey gluttons, Thanksgiving feasts, family gatherings and baking add a few more pounds to your bottom. The kick off for the Christmas shopping season blasts through the city overloading parking lots, turning kind considerate humans into warriors battling for parking spots, the last of the sale items, and their places in check out lines. The anticipation of Christmas, parties, decorations, programs and gift buying are pumping adrenaline into the kids like an air pump blows up balloons and you find yourself unable to stop and breathe because you simply just don't have the time.

Fitting in your basic curriculum requirements as well as planning arts and crafts projects, making parent's gifts, planning the school party and possibly a program takes more ingenuity than you'd ever dreamed. Then at home, you must shop for family and friends, get the tree, decorate, wrap, plan for family get togethers, try to coordinate two extended families if you're married (and want to stay that way!), two immediate families if you're divorced and even more extended families if you're remarried. Countless needy groups and organizations beg for your help and you stretch the dollar bill and that teacher paycheck (now, money doesn't matter) farther than a worn out piece of elastic could ever stretch.

Finally, three hours before Christmas day, you've found all the bargains, cooked 12 dozen cookies for the church cookie swap, baked homemade goodies for the neighbors (or bought bakery goods and wrapped them in your own aluminum foil as a disguise), hand stenciled all your own wrapping paper and wrapped all the presents, survived the school Christmas party disaster and all the other holiday havoc. You fill the tub with hot water, climb in, sit back and relax and sip on the last alka seltzer in your pantry. You actually survived the holiday havoc without having to commit yourself to one of the local mental wards although you did pick up the phone and dial the number once. Ah, the holidays are finally here. You can relax. But as you slowly sink into the warm water you feel a nagging twitch in your spine. What have you forgotten? The church party, the gift for your brother you have to mail twelve days in advance to reach him and you have only ten days left until Christmas, or is it you've forgotten how to relax!

TIPS

Plan ahead. Get organized with a calendar and lists for home and school. July isn't too early for shopping for Christmas bargains, that is unless, you thrive on last minute hurry scurry.

Get plenty of rest and try to eat properly. Also try to fit in a little exercise. You'll feel less stressed, have more energy and avoid the guilts from all that holiday snacking if you try to stay in shape.

Set realistic goals; one or two things a day to try to accomplish. Also, limit yourself to one or two entertainment parties at your house. You can't possibly have seven parties in a row and feel sane.

Check off items on your list so you can see your accomplishments.

At school, enlist the help of a group of parents. Enlist volunteers for room mothers. Meet with them early to discuss your basic plans, give them lists and let them organize parties and programs. Also let them assist on craft days.

Take shortcuts at home whenever possible. Maybe your mother made homemade wrapping paper and six dozen cookies for each neighbor, but that doesn't mean you have to. Adapt to your schedule and be reasonable. Remember, it is the thought that counts, not how much work or money you put into it.

Plan a family meeting to discuss all the holiday preparations at home and how to fit them in everybody's schedules. List and let each person choose ways to help or assign duties and responsibilities to individuals. Everyone will enjoy it more and some of the burden will be off you.

If you plan to do a school program for parents, choose a short easy one with simple easy to learn lines and costumes. Plan in advance and let parents know well in advance what costumes or props you'll need. Enlist their help but don't wait until the last minute. One or two weeks notice at holiday time may irritate and anger parents who are already bulging at the seams with *to do* lists of their own. But don't begin practicing in September for a Christmas program. You and the children will be burned out before the program date arrives. You can begin introducing songs early on though so children will have learned the words and feel comfortable with the song, but don't do it at the exclusion of other important and fun activities. You can use transitional times to practice a song or two here and there.

When teaching crafts, allow more time than you think for each project since some children are perfectionists and some are slower workers than others and will become frustrated if they have to rush. Of course, have a simple fun game, reading or quiet activity available for those who slap their project together with one swipe of a brush and a dab of glue and are ready to move on. Gear your activity toward the age group, consider the difficulty of the project, and try the project at home first. Disaster may ruin your craft time if it is too difficult, your materials fail, or your time runs out and you have no other day to finish. Allow drying time before taking home so the child doesn't spend hours perfecting a project only to have it fall completely apart on the bus. Also, always bring extra supplies for those who mess up or get frustrated. Use Tacky Craft glue which dries faster than other types. If using a hot glue gun, be sure to have a group of parents in the class to assist and speed things up. Children may lose control and your class project turn into chaos if you're trying to glue 32 reindeer with one glue gun.

Plan simple and fun games for parties and remind children to bring a big bag to take items home in.

Try to slow everyone down and discuss the real meaning of the holidays, the spirit of working and being together.

Prioritize your activities and help children learn to do this, too.

When holiday havoc has subsided and you've wished them all a happy winter break, then relax and enjoy your holidays. Winter will be gusting in soon and then there's five more months of school to work, work, work.

HOW MANY MORE DAYS 'TIL SPRING BREAK?

Just when you begin to recuperate from Christmas, forget about the craziness of the holiday havoc and you have finally moved the Christmas tree from the front porch to the recycling center, that alarm clock blasts again. You sling the warm covers to the floor, stumble into the bathroom and mumble to yourself, "How many more days until spring break?"

All the curriculum that you forced aside during holiday havoc awaits you in piles as big as mountains and you know you have about three months to cram all that knowledge into those tiny yearning for learning brains before spring fever, late night little league games, and field days capture their attention and energy.

A gust of wind slaps tree branches against the house reminding you of the long winter months ahead. Dark clouds swirl through the sky, creating the loom and doom that slaughters your cheery moods. You've saved the meat of your curriculum until now, knowing that the children will have settled down from the excitement of holidays, have matured and are thirsting for knowledge. You foresee long winter days lying ahead, days too cold to tackle the playground, giving you additional time for work and projects. You know it's time to buckle down. You slide into your work clothes, hard hat and all and study your calendar. How many days until spring break? Too many to count, you decide as you drape your coat around your shoulders, grab your plan book and battle the winter wind to get to your car.

RAIN RAMPAGES

"How many days did it rain on Noah's Ark," one of the kids asks.

"Forty days and forty nights," the Genius answers.

"Think we're going to beat that record," the complainer groans.

You nod, listening to the rain pound against the roof. Two weeks ago dark clouds hovered over the ancient trees outside. Shadows of branches hung over the ground looking like giant claws scratching away the light. That same day the kids in your class roared around the playground like maniacs and developed the jitterbug disorder that accompanies the change in barometric pressure. Bodies twitched, jumped and shook out of control by their owners and voices shattered the sound barrier with their screeching, screaming, and imitations of alien sounds.

That was two weeks ago. Now, after two full weeks of incessant rain, torturous thunder storms and tornado drills, even the do gooders and pleasers are grating on your nerves. Twenty eight soggy umbrellas lie mangled and dripping on your carpet. Drenched socks and mud coated shoes squeak across the floor in the hall and if you're stuck in one of the portable classrooms (trailers), going inside the building for lunch or restroom breaks requires an additional thirty minutes of untangling and folding umbrellas, searching for raincoats and dashing for shelter. Your quiet orderly line quickly disintegrates on day one of the monsoon and you yourself squeal and scream as you slosh your way from your trailer to the bathroom. You've developed laryngitis from trying to talk above the pounding of the rain against the tin roof of the trailer. You've caught up on the curriculum, you've played all the board games your classroom owns at least 75 times and even the Genius balks when you mention the computer.

Outdoor air, open spaces and hours of running would cure a little of the irritation spurring within the class, and if the rain doesn't let up soon, you'll need more than hormone pills to keep you from going on a rampage.

But when nature dictates and decides to water the earth, most often it has its way. The only thing left for you to do is plan and pray.

TIPS

- Plan physical activities inside. Even short ten minute breaks with simple exercises, dances, fingerplay or movement activities can release energy, tension, and rejuvenate the brain. Use records, tapes, exercise, aerobics, dances, wiggle games, nerf balls, relay races, musical chairs, and other games for fun and relaxation. Get suggestions from your P.E. teacher for favorite indoor games the children may like.

- Trade off with another teacher to give you each a break. Movies and filmstrips entertain, teach, and allow you a few minutes peace. Remember to alternate quiet and inactive activities with more physical activities to keep everyone more alert.

- Plan games or free time during regular outside time. Let children bring games, tapes, building blocks, etc. from home and share to offer the class a variety from the classroom stock.

- Have RAD time; read all day. Kids bring sleeping bags and pillows and lay down and read. Record the number of books they read. You may also want to let children choose one of these books for a book report, act out parts of a book, or group together and perform a puppet show to illustrate the book.

- Plan special projects; any project that will stimulate them and include lots of hands on activities. Suggestions; science projects or experiments, art or craft projects, plays, puppet shows, book reports, make videos, etc. Pounding clay also releases energy and fosters creativity.

- Plan a special project to go along with a book the class is reading as a group or individual projects. Use a theme and plan activities around it. For example; pirate day, pioneer day, 50's day, beach day, water day, sand play etc. Include follow up art activities relating to the story or book.

- Let children put together a musical, play, puppet show, write their own stories, practice storytelling, make art projects to display.

- Plan field trips and guest speakers during the winter months to vary interest and break the monotony.

- Plan a scavenger hunt. Divide into groups and hunt. Some groups may even make up clues for other groups. You can adapt the hunt to a theme or unit. For example, if you're studying pets, hide dog bones or biscuits with clues taped to them.

- Have movie day; make popcorn and watch a fun movie.

- Plan a social hour or half hour just for fun. Let kids relax and sit around and talk.

- Have kids invent their own game; a board game or activity game. Make and share with the class.

- Plan a woodworking project. Paint when finished.

- Learn simple dances. Choose records with directions or let the children make up a new dance and teach it to others. Practice square dancing, a line dance, or make two lines and let kids take turns dancing down the middle. You can also have them exercise to music similar to aerobics. Let different children call out directions.

- Choose a theme, study and do a project. For example; practice and put on a Circus and relate other activities around it. Plan a special trip around the world and incorporate different days to *visit* a country. Do art activities relating to the country, sample foods from the area, etc.

- Arrange, organize and label all items in your room. Let the kids help.

- Play *Guess that Sound*: place objects behind a screen, a child or you, the teacher, can make the sound and let others guess what it is.

- *Feely* Game; place objects in a bag, blindfold the child or have him close his eyes; the child can reach in the bag and feel the object, then guess what it is, or describe the object and see if the class can guess. Encourage the children to give clues such how it feels, textures, size, shape, etc.

- Play indoor games such as Drop the Handkerchief, Whose Got the Button, Musical chairs, Hot potato, indoor hopscotch, Bingo, Charades, Pictionary, Doggie Doggie Where's Your Bone?, Mother May I, Baseball (set the room up with chairs as bases, you can ask questions or use a soft nerf ball), 20 questions, I Spy, Categories, The Alphabet Game, Grocery Store.

- Read or tell a story about hats such as Caps For Sale, let kids make and decorate hats and act out the story. Bring in hats from home to decorate. Set up a pretend hat store and purchase hats. Sort and classify how many different kinds of hats you have.

- Set up tents and have camping day. Make pretend fires with paper and sticks, sing around the campfire, tell stories, eat marshmallows or make S'mores for snack.

- Have a stacking contest. Let children gather all different kinds of objects and have a stacking contest to see who can stack the most. Compare which objects stack better and why. Also compare the number of items; for example, 50 buttons stacked will not be as tall as 50 blocks.

- Take an imaginary trip. Use chairs as a bus, plane, train or boat, then talk about all the things you might see. Later draw, paint a picture or write about your trip.

- Invention: invent an animal, machine, robot, game, new cereal or food, etc. Name it, tell about it, draw or write a story about it.

- Have inside contests (individual or team relays): blow handkerchief across table, measure how far you can blow, compare or race, have bean bag throw, blow balloons across the room, walk with egg on a spoon, balance paper plate on head, hold spoon in mouth with jelly bean on end, play marbles or jacks, race like different animals such as a dog, cat, pig, turtle, rabbit, frog, caterpillar, have crawling contests, use milk jugs to catch soft balls or bean bags.

- Make up a marching band. Make your own instruments and songs. Take favorite simple songs and make up your own words using the familiar tune.

- Put on a talent show, video the children and let them watch later.

- Record children singing or talking and then play back and listen.

- Pick a partner and paint a portrait of that person.

- Shoe game: (individual or team game): each child takes off one shoe and tosses it into the middle of the pile. When you say *go* each child grabs a shoe and tries to find its owner. The first person or team with their shoes on and tied is the winner. A variation of this game is to take a shoe off and lay it in the center. While one child leaves the room, someone removes one of the shoes. Then the child enters and tries to guess which shoe was removed. You may want to limit the number of shoes for smaller kids, increase for larger kids.

- Designate special days and dress and act accordingly. For example; Backwards Day; everyone wears clothes backwards, walks backwards, writes on paper backwards, etc. Other special days could be Crazy Day, Opposite Day, Inside Out Day, specific Color Days, Animal Day, etc.

- Make and decorate paper airplanes. Fly inside. Measure how far each one flies and record.

- Use nature or food items to create art. For example; give children several vegetables or fruits (some cut in small pieces) and let them create art. Example: Green pepper creatures, potato head dolls, etc.

- Play *Freeze* or statues to music. When the music stops, children must freeze or become a statue just like they are.

- Junk boxes: have children bring in boxes of junk. Display, talk about the contents, sort and classify. They can decorate a shoe box to keep their junk collections.

- Crafts: try bubble painting, marble painting, soap, sand or salt painting, paint with Q-tips, pudding paint (finger lickin' good), make sandboxes or texture boxes out of boxes filled with sand, cornmeal, flour, rice, beans. Let children play and explore, draw designs in the different boxes, measure, etc.

- Do the limbo rock to music.

- Tye dye or decorate t-shirts. Instead of dye, fill plastic bottles with a mixture of fabric paint and water, then squirt on shirts, shoes, hats, socks, etc.

- Provide different containers and toys for water and sand play.

- Create a picture: one child draws a line on a piece of paper or the chalkboard. The next child adds something, then in turn each child adds another piece and see what you create.

- Study rain: visit the library and check out books on weather and rain. Chart, graph and compare amounts of rainfall in different areas of the country. Also conduct various experiments with water; boil, freeze, talk about and bring in and examine salt water, fresh water, pond water, etc.

- Build your own city: use blocks, legos, popsicle sticks, milk cartons or cereal boxes and make your own city. Draw the roads on a large mural and sit the houses, buildings, bridges, etc. on the mural. Draw a map of your city.

- Make class books using pictures, stories, or theme related ideas. Cut your paper in the shape of a bear, butterfly, picnic basket, etc., and write about the theme.

- Make your own puppet show, store front, or rocket ship out of a large box.

- Make mailboxes out of a shoe box. Cover with paper for the top (curved part), add a flag and the child's name. Children can write letters and messages and put in large mail box. Then one child (take turns) can deliver the mail. You can write the children letters or place surprises in the mailboxes for good behavior.

- Practice juggling plastic bowling pins, nerf balls, etc., to music.

- Set up a story train. (place chairs in a row) One child starts the story by saying a sentence. Then each child adds a sentence to the story.

- Make dioramas utilizing a theme; nature, dinosaurs, the ocean, etc.

- Make up your own dot to dot pictures. Let each child make a dot to dot, then a partner connects the dots to discover what the dots make.

- Set up a parade, choose a theme such as Presidents, careers, favorite animals, storybook characters, Easter bonnet, etc., and form a parade. You can decorate posters and chairs as floats. Be sure to video.

- For careers, set up different centers in your classroom such as doctor's office, grocery store, department store, office, artists, carpenter, etc., and let children explore and role play.

- Play Memory board game or Memory by drawing or placing several objects in front of children. Let them view for a couple of seconds, then children close their eyes, you remove one and they try to guess which one you removed.

- Play copy cat; do this with art, building blocks, actions, movements to music, etc.

- Try origami. Display.

- Play a lively record. Make up dances or movements to the music.

- Play Leap Frog. Also play Jump the Lily Pads: make lily pads out of green construction paper. You can place numbers, letters, words, math facts, sentences (whatever you're working on), on the lily pads. The child starts jumping and has to name or answer the problem on the lily pad before he or she can move to the next one.

- Play *My Bag is too Full*: each child holds or pretends to hold a bag. The first child says, "My bag is too full because I have a (whatever he chooses) monkey in it." The next child repeats what the first child said and then adds something. Go around the circle until everyone has had a turn. See how far you get before someone forgets what the others said. Later you may want the children to draw a bag and some of the things in the bag.

- Play grocery store or Store: Children take turns saying, "I have a grocery store or a toy store and in it are things that start with the letter *A*." The other children guess. You can go through the whole alphabet in order or randomly.

- Collect things from nature before and after a rain. Study and note the changes and differences that rain or moisture causes.

- Make flying saucers out of plastic lids or paper plates. Make up and draw a story about alien creatures.

- Tournaments: have tournament day; set up board game tournaments, math tournaments, spelling, new words tournaments, etc.

ADDITIONAL RESOURCES:

> Teacher resource books
> Valentine Productions Tapes: <u>Games for Rainy Days</u>
> <u>Surviving Summers With Kids</u>: *Rain, Rain Go Away*

WILL SUMMER EVER COME?

You're on your last six weeks of school and your last leg, as they say. You stare in amazement at the children that now face you as the countdown for summer begins. These children who sit before you now have not only grown two inches in size but their heads have actually swollen from all the knowledge that you have drilled, packed, poured, stuffed, crammed and molded into their skulls.

Spring break has come and gone but spring fever has infiltrated your kids from their toenails to their hair follicles. The athletes in your class sit slumped with drooping eyelids from late night ballgames and late bedtimes while the nature freaks are clutching their magnifying glasses ready to explore the great outdoors. The gymnasts are hanging like monkeys from the jungle gym and your daydreamers overlook the math papers for the flock of birds chirping on the windowsill outside your room. The beach is whispering your name and you complain, "Every year seems to get longer. I wish they'd stop adding days!"

The spring musical is a success. Field day is a disaster. Your allergies peak and thrust you into periodic sneezing attacks and the thought of another paper bag meal and drive through window spirals your stomach into spasms. Your mind is stressed out. Your body is ragged. Children seem to tug on you like waves that slap against a deserted boat. The heat drains you of life, energy and enthusiasm and although you've grown fondly attached to each and every little breathing life form in your room, you know that soon each and every one of those little bodies is getting closer to moving on. You wipe the sweat off your forehead as you watch them run wildly on the playground, then slap at a mosquito. Your mind and body as well as theirs is desperately in need of the summer break. "Will it ever come?"

CHAPTER 8

TEACHER, TEACHER
Thoughts From Children

BEFORE I STARTED SCHOOL

Before I started school I thought it was about the size of 3 mansions. I thought it was huge. I thought the lunch room served spinach sandwiches and broccoli because my big brother and sister said it was really gross. So they took their lunch everyday. I thought the teachers slept in school because there was a pillow behind my kindergarten teacher's desk and we had a loft. I thought she slept in our loft. *Emily Herron, 3rd grade*

Before they start school little kids think it would be fun. Before I started school I thought they would make me read when I didn't know how.   *Jonathan Pittard, 3rd grade*

Before I started school I thought that they were going to work all day with out any food. At my house my mom read me the story with the evil teacher that turns her students into apples so I thought that my teacher would turn me in to an apple but now I know that it is not true.   *Justin Wike, 3rd grade*

Before I started school I thought that we would have homework. And I thought that the teacher would color the chalkboard green and that if they were bad they would have to go to jail.

Katie Winterbottom, 3rd grade

When I was little I thought school would be huge and in the library there would be millions of books. I thought when my teacher was mad she would turn into a mean, mean dinosaur. I also thought that in the principal's office there would be a machine that turned bad kids into pencils because the principal has a lot of pencils.

Tiffany Reese, 3rd grade

Before I started school I thought my teacher was going to turn into a zombie and bite me in the neck. I thought she would give us homework and it was a hundred pages of it.

Jennifer Beardsley, 3rd grade

Before they start school, little kids think sometimes their teachers would hit you if you did something wrong. If you did something over and over again the teacher will turn you into an evil monster with sharp teeth and will throw you in a big, dark dungeon if you did it one more time. I was so scared the first day of kindergarten.

Chase Sutton, 3rd grade

Before I started school I thought that all the teachers that worked at the school would never go back to their homes. They would stay here, sleep here, eat here and never go back to their pets if they had some. The day right before school I dreamed that after school I couldn't find the way out and I went into a room and stayed there til dark. Lots of people were there. Then I saw there was a castle and all the people there were saying the pigs are coming out of their castles. When I tried to get out all the doors were locked. All the pigs turned into ghost and put needles in our necks.

Elizabeth Wang, 3rd grade

Before I started school I thought that my teacher was a BIG NASTY WITCH! But then I got over it. And then I thought my teacher would shrink us into pencils because my sister has a pencil with faces on it.   *Matt Reichman, 3rd grade*

Before they start school, little kids think that the teachers are mean and give lots of homework! And they think they will hurt them.

Elizabeth Van Galder, 3rd grade

Before I started school, little kids thought that teachers were crazy. When teachers stayed at school I thought they slept at school every day.   *Nathan Grider, 3rd grade*

MORE THOUGHTS FROM KIDS

I wish my teacher would let me play baseball with a real baseball and bat outside on the playground. My teacher never yells. She makes me pull a card. I like school! Don't you?

Philip Armstrong, 3rd grade

I really like my teacher when we read stories out loud. I think it's fun because everybody is reading together because it's real boring when we read alone.   *Chris McCain, 3rd grade*

My teacher looks nice. Her hair is always styled and she smells good. My teacher yells when we are noisy and when Philip is goofing off. I thought teachers wouldn't tell stories like she does. She tells the best *Mrs. Haygood stories* I ever heard. My teacher laughs a lot. She is very funny. I love my teacher. *Now, class, let's get quiet. 1,2,3, look at me.*   *Jessica Jackson, 3rd grade*

My teacher looks pretty when her hair is up. The best thing about my teacher is she is nice to me. My teacher laughs when we tell her a joke. My teacher smiles when she sees us working. My teacher sings at bus time. But the very best thing is her Famous Mrs. Haygood stories.   *Katie Cherri, 3rd grade*

My teacher looks like a famous movie star because she looks decent. We come in the class looking half way blown up. Sometimes I come in with shirts and pants that have holes in them. And sometimes we don't even brush our hair or teeth. Some of us have not even taken a bath for a week or two. And all the boys put everything on backwards like our hats.

Fabe Clements, 3rd grade

I wish my teacher would have us do more dress up book reports! They are fun because I like to dress up as a gymnast and other cool people! I would like to have rest time, too. My teacher tells great stories. She is nice but when's she's mad you're in trouble. She's very funny.   *Kaitlin M. Tronnes, 3rd grade*

When I first saw my teacher I thought my teacher was going to a be a very good teacher. When she is telling us stories, they are good. You can make one up with your own name it in. You can make up one and put it in a book and give it to your next teacher. I like her just because she is her. The best thing about my teacher is that she likes you and that's why you should respect your teacher. They care what you learn.   *Claire Kittinger, 3rd grade*

My teacher smiles when someone asks a funny question. The best thing abut her is she tells funny stores. We laugh ha-ha-ha-ha-! It is really funny. I laugh a lot. She should be an author. My teacher smiles, sings, laughs when someone is funny.   *Brian Crews*

My teacher should tell more of her famous stories to us. It's too bad every kid can't have my teacher. On the first day of school when I saw her, I thought she was beautiful. She smiles beautifully. My teacher hardly yells. She only yells when she is so mad she could burst. That has only happened once so far (thank goodness).

                                        Molly Levinson, 3rd grade

My teacher smiles when we do our work. My teacher sings when she is happy.   *Jimmy Reynolds, 3rd grade*

When I first saw my teacher I thought she was 20. She looked very calm and nice, which she is. My teacher only yells when someone argues with her, but when she is in a good mood she's really nice. And everyone seems to calm down. That's a note to you, if you are going to be a teacher.   *Katie Winterbottom, 3rd grade*

I thought my teacher was going to be mean but when I saw my teacher she was very nice. She gives us candy if we are good and if there is enough. She also tells us stories. They are special because they have us in them and we go to lots of places. There is a poem. A teacher has a special way of making learning fun, finding joy everyday, and the best in everyone. The poem is from a book.

                                        Felicity Green, 3rd grade

I wish my teacher would buy us ice cream. We get ice cream on Tuesday and Friday. All of our class likes it. Everybody likes ice cream day but we really love our teacher. Just because she does not buy us ice cream does not make us like her any less.

                                        Jesse Young, 3rd grade

I wish my teacher had drawing in more subjects. We have a lot of subjects with drawing but I just don't like what we draw. I also wish my teacher would not give us so much homework. My teacher never yells. She lets us watch films and movies a lot.

Matt Reichman, 3rd grade

My teacher sings when it is bus time. Sometimes we take a nap and she sings. I wish my teacher would give us some parties.

Susan Chung, 3rd grade

The best thing about my teacher is she is so nice to everyone. She makes spelling very easy for everyone. Instead of writing our spelling every night and studying so much we play games like hop-along spelling and Stop Sign Spelling. It is fun. I wish my teacher would always be happy and never get mad.

Emily Herron, 3rd grade

The funniest thing my teacher ever did was to glue her pants to the floor. When I was in kindergarten she got glue on her pants, then sat down and it dried. She was stuck to the floor.

Adam Herron, 9th grade

The funniest thing my teacher ever did was when she spilled borax on the carpet. She tried to clean it up so it wouldn't take the color out. *Elizabeth Herron, 5th grade*

My teacher is kind of funny when she gets sort of mad and grumpy on Fridays and she bangs her fist on the table.

Sarah Sanchez, 3th grade

The funniest thing a teacher has ever said was when my teacher said Mother Hummer (Mothaa Huma) in a country northern accent in class. *Jim Hess, 8th grade*

When I first saw my science teacher I thought she looked like a bug. *Adam Herron, 8th grade*

My favorite teacher was in third grade. When we did good things she would throw candy out to us. If we weren't listening she would squirt us with a water gun, not enough to get us really wet, just enough to get our attention. It was fun. We did lots of creative writing
                                    Daniel Olsen, 7th grade

My favorite teacher was in 9th grade. He told the class you could sleep in class, but then he's so funny that you don't want to or can't.   *Misty Olsen, 9th grade*

My worst teacher was in first grade. She never said anything positive. Once on a math test I got all the problems correct but got a zero because I chose to color the picture with different colors than the teacher specified.   *Misty Olsen*

I like my teacher because everyday she asks me if I've had my hug for the day. Then she hugs me and whispers in my ear that she loves me.   *Rebecca Odum, 2nd grade*

I hate it when my teacher gets mad at everyone and makes us all put our hands down on our desk and I didn't do anything.
                                    Rebecca Odum, 1st grade

My teacher is so funny. She calls your bottom your *bahuta* and when she wants everyone to sit in the circle she says, "Now everyone sit down on your *bahutas*."
                                Martin Minschwaner, preschool

The weirdest thing my teacher did was wear a birthday hat on her birthday. It was a pink, round, curly hat. *Michael Adams, 1st grade*

My teacher's voice sounds like a manager or an accountant like my mommy. My teacher never yells when she gets angry. She talks about it. The best part about my teacher is her nice understanding heart and her smooth voice.   *Erin Sullivan, 5th grade*

When I first saw my teacher I thought she looked like she would be very nice. For example, when I walked into the room she was all cheery. She also has a good sense of humor, but when she gets bad reports she's not too humorous.   *Wes Smith, 5th grade*

My teacher looks like....a best friend. My teacher, a cool lady, and a great brain maker. (We mixed cream of tartar, salt and flour)
Catherine Collins, 5th grade

My teacher looks like someone nice. She is beautiful. When she gets mad she doesn't really yell.   *Elizabeth Herron, 5th grade*

I wish my teacher would let us get ice cream every day and let us have a longer snack. My teacher's voice sounds like a bird's.
Johnathan Buice, 5th grade

My teacher looks like she is beautiful.   *Lauren Maki, 5th grade*

I wish my teacher would let us walk to the park everyday for lunch because I love fresh air. We could wade in the river, run around, sleep under trees, eat peacefully and walk the trails. I'm sure I'd love that.   *Beth Douglas, 5th grade*

The best part about my teacher is . . . when she tells you if your grade goes into the gradebook or not.   *Joshua Halpern, 5th grade*

I wish my teacher would take us to Six Flags and White Water and pay us money for school.   *Corey Hughes, 5th grade*

I wish my teacher would not believe in homework. I wish she would pay us to come to school. I wish my teacher would never do health. I wish my teacher always did math and science. I wish my teacher would also drive us home.   *Brandon Bush, 5th grade*

The best part about my teacher is ...she is nice, funny, sweet. She keeps us together like a mother swan and we're her ducklings. Also none of us are her favorites or her enemies. She treats us all the same.   *Jessica Blackstock, 5th grade*

TEACHER, TEACHER, WHERE ARE YOU?

"Teacher, teacher, tie my shoe."

"Teacher, teacher, I don't get this."

"Teacher, he won't leave me alone."

"Teacher, teacher, I don't feel good."

"Teacher, teacher, this is stupid."

"Teacher, teacher, not homework AGAIN!"

"Teacher, TEACHER, where are you?"

HELP! I'M UNDER THE PAPERWORK!

"Help! Somebody, help!" you scream, huffing and clawing at the desk, trying to push the mounds of papers away and forcing your head up through the sludge.

"Help, over here. I'm under the paperwork," you scream but your breath only causes the papers to flap and fly into disorder.

Your fingers crawl across the top of your desk and one of the children shrieks.

"Aaaah! It's IT from the Adam's family."

"What's going on here?" you hear the Principal's voice sift its way through the holes between the piles of papers. "Where is your teacher?"

"Here, here," you call, slapping your hands frantically. Your screams are muffled through the piles of papers and your voice sounds like a tiny whisper.

"As soon as I finish this stack, I can start class," you groan.

You claw at the papers and just as your eyes reach the top of the pile and you think you see light, someone slaps another bundle on top and you are buried again.

How can you teach and meet all those special needs when you are tied to your pen and imprisoned by truckloads of papers? Checklists, conference forms, assessments, evaluations, individual testing, group testing, forms for this, forms for that, forms for everything, referrals, IEP's, committees, attendance and state forms, lesson plans, papers to grade, the list is endless. You feel like you need a full time clerk and either you sacrifice the time with your class and do the paper work at school, or you cart the sludge pile home into your off hours. Where is the relief? You've tried aspirin and tums but even rolaids can't make it all disappear.

TIPS

Organize and stay organized. Keep not only a daily planner but a monthly planner. Set a certain time period for paperwork, perhaps a little each day and try to stay caught up instead of letting it mound up so high that you feel overwhelmed. Try to use any assistants, parents, or classroom helpers to help you get through it. Utilize family members (dependable ones such as older children) to help grade papers or complete light form work.

Make any suggestions to combine forms, paperwork, etc., that you see possible. Keep information and papers on each child in a *working* folder for ease of evaluating.

Utilize your spare moments such as sitting in carpool lines, waiting at the gym to pick up a child, even tv time to get the bulk done.

Before a particular busy or heavy paperwork time such as conferences, get your plan book in order in advance, then block off time to get the paperwork done.

BURNOUT

You've been teaching in the same room for ten years and the years seem to be running together like thin pancake syrup. You can't remember whether you did this activity already this year or was it last year? The new faces of students are blurs of ones in year's gone by. The anticipation that filled you when you first began your career has dwindled into dread and your idealism has been shattered by parents, students, and the system. When your 27 children leave your room every day, you watch for your own to walk in and they seem to get skimpy portions of your left over patience. You've forgotten how to have a conversation with adults and what it is they even discuss besides kids and school and the names Mom and Teacher are the only ones you answer to.

The thirteenth round of stomach flu killed your Florence Nightingale instincts and magically disintegrated your halo into thin air. Then your dedication trembled like the after shock of an earthquake when a parent accused you of Satanism. Your innocence and youth were zapped faster than a microwave boiling water when you heard a kindergartner tell you she was going to have sex with a friend and when the evening news report focused on the discovery of guns in one of the middle schooler's locker.

The challenge of teaching has suddenly become a chore instead of a challenge. Your aging body is sagging and the words *midlife crisis* finally make sense to you. What is going on?

You're too young for menopause, but teacher burnout, well, there's a possibility. When the words *Teacher, Teacher* start grating on your nerves like a nail scratching your best coffee table and your teaching plans become a monotonous routine, it may be time for a break.

What can you do?

Admit you may be feeling burnout. It happens to everyone in every kind of career. Teaching is demanding, stressful, and physically and mentally exhausting. If you can afford it, take a break, perhaps a year off for relaxation, time with your own family, a sabbatical, time to go back to school, or to explore options. Take fun classes or work on that Six Year or Masters degree you've always wanted to pursue.

If you can't take time off, be sure to plan time away for yourself, a vacation alone or with a spouse or friend.

Get involved in women's groups, cultural groups, craft clubs, or pursue a hobby, etc.

Force yourself to leave work at school and use your time at home for yourself.

Request a change in grade level or school. Even minor changes in your room, plans, substituting new units, reorganizing your centers, bulletin boards, behavioral charts, etc., can revitalize your interest and enthusiasm.

Attend a conference; often times the fellowship and speakers can spark that interest, reaffirm your dedication and offer you new ideas.

Offer to teach a workshop or be a speaker at a teacher's workshop. Thinking through and planning a motivational talk may stimulate you and revitalize that motivation you need.

Request a student teacher. New blood, enthusiasm, and ideas can be inspiring and motivating. You can both learn from one another and the new teacher's innocence and dedication may be what you need to rejuvenate yours.

Plan activities to release stress; exercise classes, walking, etc., (therapy!).

Form a group of friends who share your feelings; teachers or non teachers. Plan a special night out weekly or monthly.

Log the accomplishments of students and yourself and make a special celebration for them and yourself when you reach goals.

Remind yourself daily of how valuable you are, even if you aren't paid what you're worth and your salary won't cover your mortgage. Inherent in you is still that admiral quality and knowledge that somehow, someway you are making a difference in the lives of the young people of our future. Listen for that one thing, that little word, phrase or even that smile from a student that will tell you how much you're really worth. Then etch it in gold in your mind forever.

TEACHER APPRECIATION DAY:
A NATIONAL HOLIDAY

National holidays are designated for Presidents, Martin Luther King, Veterans, but what about teachers? Teachers who devote their time, love and lives to the growth and development of our future generations receive little attention except for gripe sessions from peeved parents. National Teacher Appreciation Week now exists and is recognized in May. Shouldn't teachers get the day off! Counties should make banners, have parades, write and dedicate special songs, rent a Good Year Blimp, shower teachers with gifts, and declare a National Holiday!

You may be lucky enough to teach in a school that celebrates this week in grandiose fashion or you may teach in a school that thinks teacher appreciation means the teacher telling the school system how thankful she is to have a job. Most celebrations and special activities are planned through the PTA so you may want to make some suggestions, as a parent or teacher, to make this week special, even if it can't be declared the national holiday that it should be.

SUGGESTIONS:

PTA's can organize special methods of recognizing teachers during this week through the room mothers coordinating efforts. Parents can offer their own ideas.

A parent volunteer can act as a substitute for the teacher for a portion of the day, giving her a break. The parent can carry out the teacher's plans for that time period.

Parent volunteers provide duty free lunch for staff or send special lunches in for teachers.

Organize a system where different grade levels bring special treats and snacks to the teacher's lounge during that week.

Parents can volunteer to take the class for a short time during the week and help the class make banners, posters, write poems, decorate the room, make gifts, etc., for the teacher. Coordinate this time with the teacher.

Children may bring in gifts, homemade cards, or donate money for a class gift (perhaps flowers, a plant, gift certificate for a local store or restaurant, or of course, a new tote bag!).

Schools might give each teacher a day off for Christmas shopping.

Teachers may want to issue a classroom wish list such as special books, stickers, arts and crafts items, etc. The parent may want to buy or donate these to the classroom or teacher.

TEACHER APPRECIATION DAY
Thoughts From A Few Kids:

MRS. MORGAN
by Emily Herron, 2nd grade

Mrs. Morgan, Mrs. Morgan
you are so kind
You make me think
with my own mind.
As you see
you are too nice
so I'll go home
and tell all the mice.

MRS. BYRD
by Elizabeth Herron, 4th grade

Mrs. Byrd is a great teacher!
Roses are red, violets are blue, I like you
Super teacher!

Byrd is her name and I won't forget it.!
You are nice and funny!
Reads and picks out the best books!
Does the best drawing!

Love, Elizabeth

MRS. SMITH

by Matthew Adams

My summer dream come true
Real fun way to learn
She makes me smile
She was scared to go on Ruby Falls
Marbles are a neat thing
I'll never forget her
The zoo was a blast
Happy I go to spend the year with her
Glad I'm in her class
Really liked hearing about Lindsey
Always remember 4th grade because of her
Doing poetry was amazing
Every day was so fun
4 ever my friend.

TO MRS. ROSENBERG

From James Bass II, 8 years old

POETRY

Regardless of what has come...
or what must be...
I'll never forget
your kindness to me...
If there ever comes a time
when you're sad or blue
Remember Mrs. Rosenberg...
James loves you.

MRS. BYRD

by Allison Bouknight, 4th grade

Mrs. Byrd you're the best
You're a teacher who's very well dressed
You're nothing like the rest
Liking you is not in jest.
Love, Allison

TEACHERS

by Michael A. Thomason, 4th grade

My teacher is really cool
She teaches elementary school
I really love her science
She is better than an electric APPLIANCE!

MY TEACHER

by Leah Mitchum, 4th grade

The land is green
The ocean is blue
You are the best teacher
I ever knew.
From the ocean
to the mountains
Plateau to the plains
you're the best teacher still
even when it rains.

MY TEACHER

by Amanda Lightfoot, 4th grade

Roses are red
Violets are blue
You're the best teacher
I ever knew.
You're friendly,
You're fun—
Your're MY # 1.

MY TEACHER

by Sarah Chattin, 4th grade

Here's a poem for you, Mrs. Byrd
To show my gratitude,
especially because your are a very special dude!
Thank you for all you've done
You've taught me very well
It will be easier in 5th grade because of your cool self.
Thank you, thank you, thank you for doing all you can!!!
Love, your biggest fan!

THANK YOU, TEACHER FOR:

Thank you, teacher for helping us learn about Egypt. Also thank you for teaching us about maps.   *Sarah Sanchez, 4th grade*

Thank you, teacher, for bringing a real eyeball in for science. It was neat seeing the real thing instead of drawings.

Elizabeth Herron, 5th grade

CHAPTER 9

HURRAY! SCHOOL'S OUT!

Waves of excitement fill the air, but your fuel tank is running on empty. Completing the grade level requirements, conferences, placement, testing, field days and end of the year parties have drained you of your last few drops of spunk.

Warm gentle breezes and the explosion of blooming flowers, budding trees and picnicking in the park beckon you to laziness. Daydreaming 101 overpowers your concentration on math and spelling. Thoughts of the soft lapping waves of the ocean, exploring sandy seashores, huddling in a desolate mountain cabin, the gurgling of a mountain stream, barefoot toes wiggling into ice cold river water, and the smell of honeysuckle infiltrate your nerve endings. And for a few fleeting minutes your imagination craves the stimulation of a steamy love novel instead of a children's book.

"Hurray! School's out!" you hear the children shout as they stampede towards the bus. Boxes of craft junk and stacks of half used construction paper and supplies that were once neatly stacked are now crammed into corners. Games and puzzles with missing pieces await your attention. The storage of bulletin board borders and supplies, poster games, charts, and the various asundry collection of junk you call teaching aids must be packed. You envision yourself and fellow teachers marching with banners and waving the last bus away, cheering and celebrating, but instead, you collapse into a chair, study the massive clean up that faces you, and hear yourself mumble with paralyzed fear, "One down; 24 more to go to retirement."

ONE DOWN: 24 MORE TO GO TO RETIREMENT

You count your years of experience to heighten that pay check a few dollars or are you counting the years until retirement?

You watch as the kids sling their bookbags over their backs one last time and hang on the end of their seats waiting for the bell. Flashbacks of the year surge through your mind. You must begin the laborious task of clean up, taking down bulletin boards, packing boxes and files, stripping walls, windows and doors, completing class files to store for the next teacher, and all the other trivial but necessary chores of post planning. You tried to begin the chores over the last week while also teaching but you haven't even made a dent in the pile of *to do's*.

You have one or two days to get it all done and you'll be on your way to fun in the sun, your vacation with your own kids, or perhaps that summer job that allows you to pay your bills. A little incentive there and you drag yourself up off your chair. You glance across the hall and see a couple of teachers moving faster than jet skiers. Their room is already bare, boxes are packed and it looks like a drag race in the hall with teachers pushing boxes and battling over the only roll away cart to carry the hordes of teacher paraphernalia they've collected over 25 years. You learned not to question intentions for the wide assortment of things teachers collect because you know there will be a purpose or use for each item, no matter how strange or bizarre it might seem. You've had a few weird ideas yourself this last year.

Your first instinct is to rake the shelves and items into a big box and label *to be sorted another day* but your better judgment tells you to organize a little as you go. When you've loaded your entourage and slapped your foot on the gas pedal, your daydreams and vacation plans may overcome your *good sense* and that school room may be temporarily forgotten. Out of sight, out of mind and that *other day* may never come.

TIPS

First, if possible, find out if you'll be in the same room the next year. If you are, you may be able to store things there. If not, you'll definitely need to pack everything and perhaps you can go ahead and move some things to your new space.

Before school is out, begin organizing and cleaning out files. It's better to sort your files as you finish them, keeping one good copy of each page or idea and chucking the rest. Utilize any helpers, para pros, etc., to help finish these tasks.

When you finish a unit, file all the material and ideas you discovered to go with it in one file. You may think you'll remember which books you read last year on the subject of Egypt, but you won't.

Label everything for ease of finding the next year. Keep copies of any type of form you use, supply and inventory forms, notes to parents, etc. Keep a master copy of where you store all items and supplies, especially if some are housed in different closets in the school, the library, etc.

Organize bulletin board and art materials according to months, seasons, and units. Keep a master file or list for ease of finding what you have. (Especially for items like poster games, box games, etc. that won't fit into a file folder.)

At home designate a special area for storing teacher material, a closet, attic or corner of the basement and keep all together. Use large boxes that poster board comes in (grocery stores and department stores will give them away when they are empty) to store poster games, bulletin board materials, etc.

End your year on a positive note and think of all the progress and growth accomplishments you have made as a teacher as well as the progress, growth and accomplishments of your class.

And finally, as you chalk one year down and begin to count towards your retirement, remember that your value certainly is much higher than your paycheck. You've accomplished a marvelous feat both for yourself and the children you teach, so pat yourself on the back. Good things come in little pieces, but it's often the little things that are the sweetest. So, teachers, you survived the year. Now Stand Up and Be Counted!

SAYING GOODBYE IS NEVER EASY, BUT IT'S THE RIGHT THING TO DO

Tears sting your eyes and the lump in your throat sits like clay. Little arms cling to you and whispers of *I'll miss you, teacher* stab at your heart. Wasn't it only yesterday that your pried those arms off the child's mother and carried him into your room, struggling and crying and unsure of himself? Then trust finally came and you felt exhilarated at each tiny accomplishment he made.

Saying good bye is never easy, as the song says, but it's the right thing to do. Although goodbye isn't forever, you may feel like you have an empty nest when that last little grimy foot shuffles out the door.

After weeks of trying every bag of tricks you know, you wanted to celebrate when Jason finally read his first word. And when Stephanie babbled her first book report after being so nervous that she threw up twice, you felt your stomach quiver, too.

Whether it's on to another teacher or even another school, farewells tug at your emotions like you tug at a new pair of panty-hose and some of your students may be juggling their feelings with egg shells for hands.

So before the roller coaster of emotions zips though your room and crashes, shattering you and your kids into screams and tears, remember to pave the way for a smoother ride.

TIPS

Expect that farewells pose a harder and more difficult emotional transition for some children than others and although you don't play favorites, some children will undoubtedly touch special nerve endings and a permanent place in your heart.

Keep a photo album throughout the year for you and the children to follow events and progress of the year. Point out changes and growth.

Focus on positive changes and growth.

Focus on specific ways the children are ready for the next year and help them to feel good about it. To make the transition smoother, refer to them as *Rising 2nd graders or 3rd graders* and have a mock day where they pretend they are in the next grade. Set up your class as this grade. For example; if you teach kindergarten, have one day designated as *First Grade Day* and set the class up and your schedule to imitate a day in first grade. Give them a sample of the work and schedule of a typical day. This will get them excited. Also show them some of the books or materials they might be using so they'll have something to look forward to. Visit the class (grade) they will be going into, if possible.

Role play situations of change and help the children discuss feelings. Try to help them alleviate fears.

Remind the class to come by your room and visit, see you in the hall, etc.

Give out your phone number to those who may seem to have difficulties and who might want to call you over the summer.

Let the children stencil or stamp small pieces of paper to make stationery. They can write you a note over the summer and mail it to you.

Have children write about their feelings, both about the school year, the summer and their anticipation of the next year. You may want to list some ideas, for example: *Things I Liked This Year, Things I Didn't Like, What I Wonder About Next Year*, etc.

Plan a special fun program or farewell party at the end of the year to give the children something to look forward to and a pleasant memory to end the year on.

Plan an autographing party. Each child can make his own book by stapling small pieces of construction paper together. Children can sign individual pages and include their phone numbers if they wish.

Plan a class get together over the summer at a park or pool just for fun.

Make and keep a *memory book* throughout the year. Include pictures and notes about different activities the class did over the year. Date each entry. Also, have each child keep a journal or memory book to record events in as the year progresses. You may want to make a time line and display in the class.

BUGS, MUGS, JUGS, AND HUGS

Bugs of any shape, size or kind appliquéd on shirts, aprons and tote bags, 735 mugs that say #1 Teacher and jugs of cheap perfume from dollar stores will be among the glorious gifts you receive for your hours of chalkboard duty, eye strain, lecturing, cajoling, teaching, wiping noses, tying shoes, tutoring and last but not least, all your smiles and hugs. Just because you wear jumpers with apples stitched on the front, earrings that look like bunnies and shoes painted like watermelons doesn't mean you will appreciate aluminum foil headbands or pop bead necklaces, but you may get them. You laugh when you open the box of candy with the piece missing and the little boy looks up at you with guilty eyes. Then he embraces you and you know that it isn't the gift but the hugs from sticky fingers, jelly splattered faces and muddy t-shirts that are really your gifts; the hugs from the heart.

WORST GIFTS TEACHERS HAVE GOTTEN

Plastic jewelry from a dime store

Box of candy with a piece missing

An empty box

Ten identical *Teacher 1985* ornaments the same day

NICEST GIFTS TEACHERS HAVE GOTTEN

Gifts made by the children; magnets, ornaments, etc.

Ornaments

Stationery and note cards

Markers or art supplies

Books

Calendars

Home made goodies in decorative basket, jar, or container

Baskets filled with assorted items such as candy, fruit, bath items and toiletries, etc.

Puppets, games or books for the classroom

Teacher resource books or materials such as different kinds of pads (available at teacher resource centers, such as animals, fruits, etc., great for writing notes or making into centers)

Learning centers (homemade or bought)

Gift certificates (department stores, teacher supply stores, hairdresser, etc.)

Lunches (gift certificates for local restaurant)

Flowers, plants, hanging baskets, etc.

Picture frames

Vases

Small jewelry boxes

Soaps and powders for a bath room

Photo book for the class to keep pictures in

Collectibles

Holiday decorations
Holiday towels
Bath towels
Magazine subscription

TIPS

Teachers, you may want to put out a wish list. Include any thing you collect or items you'd like for the classroom such as books, globes, games, stencils, records or tapes, stickers, colored file folders, markers, storage containers, etc.

GOOD THINGS COME IN LITTLE PACKAGES

"Teacher, you're beautiful. Did you paint those lines on your face by your eyes?" a five year old exclaims.

"Class, now we're going to choose our centers. Which center would you like?"
A child frantically waves his hand. "Teacher, my mom says we're all sinners."

"Teacher, I know it's your birthday but you don't look that old, not as old as my Grandma."

"Teacher, I like your fancy clothes."

"Teacher, are your fingernails real?"

Teacher, where did you learn so much?"

"Teacher, do you sleep here at night?"

"Teacher, my grandpa can take his teeth out. Can you do that?"

"Teacher, your chest looks like a pillow."

"Class, today we're going to study prisms. Yes, son."
"Teacher, I've seen a prism before."
"You have? Where?"
"Well, we went to see my uncle in prison last year."

"Class, today we're going to take our trip around the world."
"Teacher, my mom said I can't go, not on an airplane without her."
"It's a pretend trip."

"Teacher, Bobby said you don't know how to spit. I can teach you."
"NO, I said I don't allow spitting."

"Teacher, you don't yell too much for a teacher."

"Class, today we're going to talk about sets."
"Teacher, I already know about sex. I saw it on TV."

Kids are spontaneous, creative, imaginative, demanding and exhausting. But every parent and every teacher needs to record those cute *little things* that children say and do, those things that touch your heart, make you chuckle and force you to realize, that yes, good things come in little packages, sometimes piece by piece.

POST PARTUM BLUES

The room sits empty and organized into nice neat areas. The walls are bare, stripped of the life and vitality of the school year. The files are packed and the boxes are stacked. All the anticipation and excitement of the school year has ended and you suddenly feel the quiet that strikes after the storm. The labor has ceased, the babies are delivered and your job for the year is done. You've given birth to a class and you may feel post partum blues setting in. You're elated, proud and happy but sentiment may transform you into a misty eyed mush without any warning.

When post partum blues set in, it's time to take your vacation, bask in the sun, read trashy sex novels, eat nachos and drink beer and try to survive the summer with your own kids. On the other hand you may choose to travel, immerse yourself in worldly activities, take that Karate class you've been dying to enroll in, or plunge into a summer job such as selling sexy lingerie at Frederick's of Hollywood. Or you can lie in bed until noon.

Whatever you do, you squeeze in a week to reorganize your files and make a few new centers and bulletin board materials. But most of all do try to relax, rejuvenate yourself and completely take your mind off teaching. You'll need it just to refresh yourself because the summer months tick by quickly and before long you know you'll be pregnant again.

PREGNANT AGAIN

Bikini tan lines, solar energy, and those lazy hazy days of summer drip enthusiasm back into your system like an IV. One class moves on and as soon as you have learned to relax for the summer, lost the baby fat and spotted your toes, you find yourself barefoot and pregnant again.

A class of new babies will soon fill your room and begin their nine month growth. You'll wave to students from last years class and marvel over how big they've gotten. They're walking now, on to another teacher, another stage, and you played a big part in that growth. You'll once again feel the anxiety, the stress, the excitement and the anticipation of a new year. Blank bulletin boards, an empty plan book and the challenge of a new set of faces graze at your fingertips. After all, you're a teacher and that excitement, that challenge, those mugs and hugs that make you come back year after year are beckoning you. The smell of the chalk dust, the boxes of creative junk, and the peering questioning wondering eyes of new kids are screaming your name. And this class, it will be different from the last. You'll have new faces to learn, new names, new personalities, new challenges, new problems, and all the frustrations and rewards that come with the job. Your rumbling stomach retches in anxiety but your veins blaze with fresh blood, spiraling and churning through your body for the new gift of life you're holding inside of you: the gift of knowledge and love you have chosen to deliver.

So, teachers, grab that plan book, those files, and that tote bag and remember that teaching is filled with joys and pitfalls, so take charge now, you can survive the classroom. The rewards that you pass on may seem unnoticed but deep down isnide you know that they aren't. That is the reason you were called to teach.

SUGGESTED RESOURCES

Below is a list of suggested resources. Depending on the age and subjects you teach you will find a wide variety of books and resources available in educational stores and school supply stores.

ART

Children and Scissors, A Developmental Approach

Craft Fun by Janet McCarty & Betty Peterson, publ. by Golden Press

The Education Center: *Big Collection of Teacher Tips* (Vol. 1 & 2)
Big Book of Patterns (books 1-3)
Jumbo Patterns

Experimenting With Art by Shirley Wolfersperger & Eloise Carlston, Good Year Books

3 D Art Projects That Teach by Kids Stuff

Happy Hands & Feet

I Can Make a Rainbow by Marjorie Frank, Incentive Publ.

Instructor's Big Seasonal Arts & Crafts Book

Kids Create by Laurie Carlson, Williamson Publ.

Literature-Based Art Series from Creative Teaching Press

Little Fingers by Dale Seymour Publ.

Multicultural Art Activities by Creative Teaching Press

Puddles & Wings & Grapevine Swings by Marjorie Frank & Imogene Forte

Scissor Skills, publ. American Teaching Aids

September Patterns, Projects and Plans (other months available)

Sky Blue, Grass Green by Susan Kropa, A Good Apple Back

Small Projects for Small Hands

Things To Do With Nature's Treasures by Incentive Publ.

Totline: Toddler Theme-A-Saurus by Jean Warren

1-2-3 Art by Jean Warren

What to Do With a Squirt of Glue by Lori Howard, Kids Stuff

Your Own Thing by Lynn Molyneux, Publ. by Trellis Books

ACTIVITIES

Teachers Bag of Tricks by Patty Nelson, Incentive Publ.

Toddlers Learn By Doing by Rita Schrank, Humanics Limited

Workjobs by Mary Baratta-Lorton, Addison Wesley Publ.

BULLETIN BOARDS

Instructor's Blockbuster Bulletin Boards

The Biggest Holiday Book Ever by Patti Janet & Carson Dellosa

The Education Center's *Bulletin Boards Kids Can Make*
The Best of the Mailbox
Bulletin Boards for Busy Teachers

Everyday Bulletin Boards by the Building Blocks Publ.

Bulletin Boards for Reinforcing Positive Behavior by Lee Canter's
Associate

A Good Year Book *Big Bulletin Boards*

Hand-Shaped Art (Bulletin Boards), by Diane Bonica, A Good
Apple Book

Holiday and Seasonal Bulletin Boards, A Frank Schaffer Publ.

Bulletin Board Smorgasboard by Susanne Glover & Georgeann
Grewl, publ. by the Learning Works

Seasonal Bulletin Boards by Evan-Moor Publ.

Bulletin Board Magic by Carson Dellosa

The Big Fearon Bulletin Board Book

HOMEWORK

Lee Canter Resource Center:
  Homework without Tears for Teachers
  Homework Organizer
  Plan Book
  Creative Homework
  Homework Motivators
  Practice Homework
  Write Better Book Reports
  Use the Library

Frank Schaffer's Homework Center (Series): *Homework Helpers*

LANGUAGE, LITERATURE BASED, AND READING

A to Z With Books & Me by Imogene Forte, Publ. by Kids Stuff

Evan-Moor Corp. unit series and reproducibles

Instructor Books: *Instructor's Language Unlimited* by Diane Hellriegel

Integrating the Literature of Judy Blume in the Classroom, A Good Apple Book

The Kids' Stuff Book of Reading & Language Arts for the Primary Grades by Imogene Forte and Joy MacKenzie, publ. by Kids Stuff

Learning Magazines Day by Day All-Year-Long Book by Carson Dellosa

Literature-Based Reading, publ. by Instructional Fair, Inc.

Literature Library, a Frank Schaffer Publ.

Making Big Books With Children (Resource Book and Reproducible Patterns) by Jo Ellen Moore, Joy Evans, and Kathleen Morgan, publ. by Evan-Moor (series)

Managing the Whole Language Classroom (K-6), Creative Teaching Press

The Story Skills Series, A Good Apple Publ.

Story Stretchers (volumes 1-3), by Shirley C. Raines & Robert J. Canaly, publ. Gryphon House

Thematic unit series by Teacher Created Materials (series, example: *Penguins, Creepy Crawlers, Our Environment and others*)

Using Big Books With Children (reproducibles) by Teacher Created Materials, Inc.

COOKING

BookCooks

Cooking Up a Story by Carol Elaine Catron & Barbara Parks, Publ. by T.S. Denison

Jell-o Kids Cooking Fun publ. by Publications International, Ltd.

The Pillsbury Doughboy's Kids Cookbook, publ. by Doubleday

GENERAL (HUMOR)

REVENGE in the Classroom by Kent Grimsley, Publ. by R & E Publ.

Up the Down Staircase by Bel Kaufman

MATH

Coupon Math by Carson-Dellosa

Hands on Math, The Educational Center

Instructional Fair File Folder Math Activities

Integrating Beginning Math & Literature by Carol Rommell

Maths At Play by Linn Maskell, publ. by Dellasta Pty. Ltd.

Mathematics Their Way by Mary Baratta-Lorton, Addison Wesley

Stick Out Your Neck Series

The Education Center's Math Shape Folders

Totline 1-2-3 Math by Jean Warren

We Love Maths by Anne Morrell & Susan Stanjnko, publ. by Dellasta Pty. Ltd.

RESOURCE

Avoiding Burnout by Paula Jorde-Bloom, Publ. by New Horizons

Brainstorms Creative Problem Solving by Thomas Turner, Scott Foresman

Channels to Children by Carol Beckman, Roberta Simmons, and Nancy Thomas, publ. Channels to Children

Every Day In Every Way by Cynthia Holley & Farady Burditt, publ. by Fearon

Gifted Preschoolers, Planning Guide to the Preschool Curriculum

The Gifted Program Handbook by Dale Seymour Publ.

Handbook for Middle School Teaching, Scott Foresman

Hayes Publ. series activity books, middle school

Instructor's Teaching Kids to Care

Learning Games Without Losers by Sarah Liu & Mary Lou Vittitou, publ. by Kids Stuff

Milliken Series - reproducibles

A Planning Guide to the Preschool Curriculum, Kaplan Press

Noteworthy News, About Your Child, pre printed pads
    Preprinted name plates by Eureka
    Name tags by Trend Enterprises, Inc.
    Pre-made cut outs, *Doodles*

Novel Notes by Carson-Dellosa

Note pads by Teacher Created Materials

The Preschool Letter & Notes to Parents Book, publ. by Gryphon House

Play Together Grow Together, The Mailman Family Press

Shortcuts for Teachers by Jean Enk & Meg Hendricks, publ. by Fearon

Stick Out Your Neck Series File Folder Games

Survival Kit for Teachers & Parents, Good Year Books

Thinking Games to Play With Your Child by Cheryl Tuttle, M.Ed. & Penny Paquette

Vanilla Manilla File Folder Games by Jane Caballero

NATURE, SCIENCE AND SOCIAL STUDIES

All About Science Fairs, Teacher Created Materials

50 Simple Things You Can Do To Save the Earth by The Earthworks Group

Basic Skill Series by Instructional Fair

Careers & You by Mark Twain Media/ Carson-Dellosa

Creative Hands-On Science Cards & Activities, a Good Apple Publ.

Exciting Things to Do With Nature Materials by Judy Allen

Milliken Publ. (*Our Global Universe: A Cultural Resources Guide*) series

Mudpies to Magnets and More Mudpies to Magpies, publ. by Gryphon House, by Robert Williams, Robert Rockwell & Elizabeth Sherwood

The Table Top Learning Series: Science Fun, Rainbow Fun, Backyard, Rainy Day, Cookbook

Sift & Shout, Sand Play Activities for Children 1-6 by Kaplan Press

Kaplan: *Waterworks*

Using Recyclables for Arts & Crafts

Sniffen Count Books: Ecology Journal, Let's Get's Down to Earth

Social Studies & Science Series of Activity Books by Mark Twain Media Publ. Co.

Small World Celebrations by Jean Warren & Elizabeth McKinnon, Totline

Science Fair Projects by Instructional Fair

Science Fairs with Style, A Good Apple Book

Science on a Shoestring by Herb Strongin

All About Science Fairs, Teacher Created Materials

Creative Hands On Science Cards & Activities, A Good Apple Book

STORYTELLING

Cut and Color Flannel Board Stories publ. by T.S. Denison

Terry Jones Fairy Tales by Michael Foreman, a Puffin Book

Favorite Folktales from around the World edited by Jane Yolen

Fee Fie Fo Fum by Carol Taylor Bond, Gryphon House

Hey! Listen to This (Stories to Read Aloud), Edited by Jim Trelease

Mini-Mini Musicals by Jean Warren, Totline Teaching Tales

Rhymes for Fingers and Flannelboards , McGraw-Hill

Storytelling with the Flannel Board, T.S. Denison

Telling Stories Together, T.S. Denison

WRITING

The Creative Writing Handbook, Good Year Books

Kids Stuff: *Complete Writing Lessons*

Writing & Art Go Hand In Hand

Evan Moor: *Write Everyday*

Storybook Characters

Writing Poetry for Children

Fearon Teacher Aids: *Writer's Triangle*

Teaching Creative Writing by Melissa Donovan, A Good Apple Book

The Education Center's Writing Shape Folders (series)

Highlights Handbook Creative Writing Activities

Writing for Kids by Carol Benjamin

THE TEACHER'S DIARY

JANUARY

The Best of the Best

The Worst of the Worst

Better Luck Next Time (goals):

I DID IT (accomplishments):

FEBRUARY

The Best of the Best

The Worst of the Worst

Better Luck Next Time (goals):

I DID IT (accomplishments):

MARCH

The Best of the Best

The Worst of the Worst

Better Luck Next Time (goals):

I DID IT (accomplishments):

APRIL

The Best of the Best

The Worst of the Worst

Better Luck Next Time (goals):

I DID IT (accomplishments):

MAY

The Best of the Best

The Worst of the Worst

Better Luck Next Time (goals):

I DID IT (accomplishments):

JUNE

The Best of the Best

The Worst of the Worst

Better Luck Next Time (goals):

I DID IT (accomplishments):

JULY

The Best of the Best

The Worst of the Worst

Better Luck Next Time (goals):

I DID IT (accomplishments):

AUGUST

The Best of the Best

The Worst of the Worst

Better Luck Next Time (goals):

I DID IT (accomplishments):

SEPTEMBER

The Best of the Best

The Worst of the Worst

Better Luck Next Time (goals):

I DID IT (accomplishments):

OCTOBER

The Best of the Best

The Worst of the Worst

Better Luck Next Time (goals):

I DID IT (accomplishments):

NOVEMBER

The Best of the Best

The Worst of the Worst

Better Luck Next Time (goals):

I DID IT (accomplishments):

DECEMBER

The Best of the Best

The Worst of the Worst

Better Luck Next Time (goals):

I DID IT (accomplishments):

ABOUT THE AUTHOR

Rita Herron is a native of Atlanta and graduated from the University of Georgia with a degree in Early Childhood Education. She has taught kindergarten both in private and public schools and is a workshop leader for teachers and parents. She is a professional storyteller for children, telling both familiar stories as well as ones she has written. She is the Special Events Coordinator for the Society of Children's Bookwriters in the Alabama/Georgia region and belongs to several writer's organizations.

Her first book, *Surviving Summers with Kids: Fun Filled Activities for All*, was published in 1993.

She lives with her husband and three children in Norcross, GA.

ABOUT THE ILLUSTRATOR

Clyde Carver is a native of Atlanta and holds a Bachelor of Visual Arts/Graphics Art from Georgia State University. He has been drawing since the age of six when his first drawing of whales with a black crayon was published for a Valentine page. Clyde works for the Atlanta Journal and Constitution, does freelance illustrations and illustrated *Surviving Summers with Kids: FunFilled Activities for All*. In the future, he wants to do editorial cartoons.